G. Bernard Shaw.

Leslie Henson

Marie Rambert

Richard Buckle

Ralph Richardson

Maggie Smith

W.C. Macready

A. Tamburini

Tamara Karsavina

J. Garrick

Clara Butt.

Nellie Melba.

The Theatre Museum

Victoria and Albert Museum

Compiled by
Alexander Schouvaloff

Preface and Introduction
by
Catherine Haill

Scala Books

Joseph Grimaldi (1778–1837)
in the costume of Scaramouche

Grimaldi, the funniest of clowns, as the *commedia dell'arte* character Scaramouche or 'little skirmisher' who fears nothing except danger.

Hand coloured lithograph
Harry R. Beard Collection
HRB F67–17 CT6104

Text and captions © 1987, Alexander Schouvaloff
Illustrations © 1987, The Victoria and Albert Museum

First published in 1987 by Scala Publications Ltd
26, Litchfield Street, London WC2H 9NJ

Distributed in the USA by Harper & Row, Publishers
10 East 53rd Street, New York, NY 10022

ISBN 1 870248 03 1 (paperback)
ISBN 1 870248 04 X (UK hardback)
ISBN 0 935748 76 8 (US hardback)
LC 87–060275

Edited by Kathy Elgin
Designed by Rupert Kirby for Kirby-Sessions Design Partnership
Produced by Scala Publications
Filmset by August Filmsetting, England
Printed and bound in Italy by Graphicom, Vicenza

—ACKNOWLEDGEMENTS—

Our first and greatest thanks are to Monsieur Erté not only for designing our poster but also for so generously allowing us to use his design for the cover of this book. His marvellous drawing captures perfectly the spirit and atmosphere of the Theatre Museum.

We should also like to thank Mr and Mrs Estorick, Mrs John Vickers, Daria Borghese and our colleagues Lin Barkass, Claire Browne, Wendy Fisher, Sue Gowenlock, Naomi Joshi, Leela Meinartas, Janet Steen, Jim Fowler and Graham Brandon, who took many of the photographs, for all their help; and our special thanks also to Kathy Elgin, our editor, for her sharp eyes, patience and perceptive suggestions and to Rupert Kirby, our designer, for his sympathetic and sensitive understanding of theatrical objects.

But, above all, we are particularly grateful and indebted to Sarah C. Woodcock for all the immensely valuable and significant contributions she made and the untiring additional work she did during the preparation of this book.

Unless otherwise stated, all illustrations are from the Enthoven Collection.

Back Cover
Poster design for the 'farewell' performance by John Martin Harvey as Sydney Carton and his wife Nina (Angelina Helena) de Silva (1869–1949) in *The Only Way*, an adaptation by F. Wills of Charles Dickens' novel *A Tale of Two Cities*.

Oil painting on plywood by Charles A. Buchel
Given by Mrs Brooke-Booth
S.1131–1986

CONTENTS

PREFACE

Theatre is magical and alive. Theatre is performance – all sorts of performance – opera and pantomime, music-hall and ballet, circus and variety, magic and mime. Theatre is the expectant hush when the lights are dimmed, red plush seats and ice-cream in the interval, the familiar arias, the spectacular solo, 'a good night out'. It is laughter provoked by the pantomime Dame, outrage when Othello kills Desdemona. Theatre is Peter Pan making children believe they can fly.

Memorabilia associated with entertainment has always been special and evocative. Theatre-goers keep their programmes, their tickets and souvenirs, while objects associated with famous acts or actors have often been carefully handed down. The sword that was used by Kean was given to Irving; the mirror used by Réjane was treasured by Peggy Ashcroft; the ballet shoe signed by Fonteyn is prized by the balletomane. When live spectacle was the only form of entertainment, performers could receive the adulation granted to pop stars and film stars today. Prints and souvenirs of actors and productions were sold by the thousand, long before the camera went to the theatre. Performance is immediate but ephemeral, and yet so much careful preparation is involved – the set and costume designs, the prompt books, the sound and lighting plots, the wig and property making, the set models and backcloths. Enthusiasts over the years have preserved these items and have generously given them to the museum. Through these images and objects, the Theatre Museum hopes to transmit some of the memories and magic, the pleasure and joy of performance.

'The art of the theatre is the art of acting, first, last, and all the time.' – Harley Granville-Barker's words sum it up. This book is not another history of the theatre. Nor is it a catalogue of objects. A glimpse into one of the richest theatrical collections in the world, it is a scrapbook of images from the museum concentrating on actors, on acting. It recalls great performances we might have seen and others that are legendary. It is dedicated to all entertainers and those involved in entertainment, to all audiences and collectors who have lavishly given or bequeathed to the museum. It is dedicated to all those who strove to ensure that there should be a Theatre Museum.

Fan, c.1850, which belonged to the ballerina Marie Taglioni (1804–1884)

Cyril Beaumont Bequest
S.254–1979 CT7223

THE THEATRE MUSEUM

'Patience, after all, has characterised
this movement all along ...'
The Times, May 1957

Admission ticket to Hanover Square Concert Hall

Engraving, late 18th century, GG6241

The Theatre Museum, a branch of the Victoria and Albert Museum, is a collection of collections relating to the history of live entertainment. It came into being officially on 16 September 1974. It opened in its own premises in Covent Garden on 23 April 1987. But its story began over seventy years before.

In November 1911 the newspaper *The Referee* published a letter requesting the attention of the public to be drawn to a scheme for 'the establishment of a comprehensive theatrical section in some London museum'. Its author was Mrs Gabrielle Enthoven, an elegant and handsome woman whose great passion for the theatre was matched by her devotion to the accumulation of theatrical memorabilia. Born in 1868, she had begun her collection during the late nineteenth century and had amassed a remarkable archive of playbills, programmes, engravings, designs, drawings, photographs, press-cuttings, prompt scripts, letters and books, all relating to the history of the London stage. Her ideas received much support from the public and the profession, the actress Ellen Terry telling *The Stage* in 1911 that she would like to see it as 'a thing apart, a museum devoted only to the Drama'. Mrs Enthoven felt so strongly that such an archive should remain in Britain that she offered her entire collection as a gift to the newly-formed London Museum, refusing all foreign offers of purchase. After considerable correspondence the museum decided that they did not have the space to house the collection, replying regretfully that 'there were many other sides of London life that had prior claim'. Mrs Enthoven was disappointed. She was also undeterred.

In 1922 the Victoria and Albert Museum was persuaded to bring over from Amsterdam the successful and influential International Theatre Exhibition. One hundred and sixty-one theatre designers from eleven countries were represented with eight hundred and fifty-four objects. It was the most comprehensive exhibition of theatre design yet staged. Edward Gordon Craig, innovator and philosopher of the theatre, wrote the foreword to the catalogue. Cecil Harcourt Smith, then Director of the V & A, noted in the introduction: 'The Museum is the officially constituted centre and home for all branches of Industrial Art and Design, and there is, obviously, no branch of Art covering quite so wide a field as the Theatre, which

'I wish I hadn't bought the tickets!'

Caricature on the misuse of benefit performances by double booking.

Hand coloured aquatint, 1826
Harry R. Beard Collection
HRB F121–36 CT3787

touches Architecture, Painting, Design and Decoration in many forms.' It was clear that at least one museum in London was sympathetic towards the art of the theatre. Mrs Enthoven offered her collection to the Victoria and Albert Museum. In March 1924 it was accepted.

Mrs Enthoven continued working on her archive at the museum, giving not only her services but also, initially, funds to pay for some assistance. As she told a reporter from the *Evening Standard* in 1924: 'My object is not to collect curiosities but to make a collection which will be of value in affording reliable material for the art of the theatre and for theatrical history. I am continuing the collection of modern playbills, programmes and photographs.' The war interrupted all museum activities in London, but when the collections were returned to the capital a young Museum Assistant, George Nash, was detailed to help Mrs Enthoven. In 1950 Mrs Enthoven died but George Nash continued to maintain the collection until his retirement in 1978, developing an unrivalled knowledge of the collection. Mr Nash retired before the opening of the new museum, but the collection that he worked on with its founder continues to grow. Expanded to cover all professional performances in Great Britain, it provides essential source material from which all theatrical research begins.

The Theatre Museum owes much to the persistence and dedication of many individuals. It also owes much to the newspapers who ensured that their views became matters of public debate. In 1911 *The Referee* had published the letter from Mrs Enthoven. In 1955 *The Times* published one from Laurence Irving, grandson of the great actor-manager Sir Henry Irving. The letter expressed his concern that so many theatrical treasures were leaving the country. He urged that the exodus be halted, asking: 'Is it not time that in the native land of the greatest dramatist the world has known and of actors and actresses of incomparable genius a theatrical museum worthy of them is established?' His worry was shared by many others who joined in the correspondence with alacrity. Fortunately, Irving's rhetorical question was not ignored. The Society for Theatre Research had been in existence since 1948, and with the help of the Arts Council the Society founded The British Theatre Museum Association in May 1957. Laurence Irving was appointed as Chairman and *The Times* reported the inaugural meeting of the Association at the Theatre Royal Drury Lane, noting: 'No-one supposed that permanent premises for the museum could be come upon just around the corner. Patience, after all, has characterised this movement all along, for it is getting on for two years since Mr Laurence Irving started it with his letter to *The Times* urging the need for a central and comprehensive collection of theatrical art.' The need for patience was prophetic but indeed, thirty years later the museum did open in permanent premises just around the corner from Drury Lane Theatre!

The main concern of the newly-formed British Theatre Museum Association was to attract gifts and bequests of theatrical material, as well as increased membership and funds. Donations to the Association began to arrive in response to newspaper articles headed: 'You Can Help The Theatre Museum', 'Theatre Museum Seeks Relics' and 'Museum For Theatreland'. There were no premises for their collection, but all gifts were gratefully acknowledged by the honorary curator, G.B.L. Wilson – known to everyone as 'G.B.'. Meanwhile, Committee members stored the boxes and packages in every available corner of their homes. Small gifts were as gleefully received as the larger archives including that relating to Sir Henry Irving, donated by Laurence Irving, and the Ivor Novello collection. With more material to display, the need for a home in which to display it became ever more urgent. In December 1962 the actor Donald Sinden – a recently appointed committee member – told the press with characteristic enthusiasm that suitable premises were likely to become available 'and that would make 1962 a theatrically historic year indeed.'

In June 1963 the *Guardian* was able to report: 'Seven years of hard work have at last produced a British Theatre Museum which is to open on June 18 at Leighton House in Kensington. The public will be admitted on Tuesdays, Thursdays and Saturdays and the organisers hope that their collection will become the nucleus of a National Theatre Museum.' Generous grants from Neville Blond, the Coulthurst Trust, and later Lord Delfont, made it possible for the Association to rent the former childrens' library from Kensington Council at a nominal rent. Sir Hugh Casson gave his services to design the interior of the museum, which was opened by the actress Vanessa Redgrave. The Association had won a battle, but they were still fighting the war. Laurence Irving made this fact clear in his opening address: 'The purpose of the show-room is to call attention to the need for a permanent British Theatre Museum to be established not by this or by any other association, but by the Government.' He emphasised that once this had happened, the British Theatre Museum Association would close. Its work would have been completed.

In many ways the British Theatre Museum was too successful. The Association had installed their collections in premises, however small, and had secured enough privately-raised funds to appoint Jennifer Aylmer as curator (succeeding G.B.L. Wilson and Freda Gaye), and Jean Scott-Rogers as Administrator. Their collections grew magnificently, but so did the cost of their maintenance. In February 1967 the museum was threatened with closure due to lack of money. *The Times* published a letter deploring the probable closure, stating: 'This is not a case for renewed support for private generosity. We feel that the museum should be taken over by the appropriate Government department and maintained in a manner analogous to, for example, the National Maritime Museum.' The letter was signed by Peggy Ashcroft, Hugh Beaumont, Edith Evans, William Gaskill, John Gielgud, Peter Hall, Harold Hobson, Allardyce Nicoll, John Osborne, Ralph Richardson, and B.A. Young. In March, members of Parliament supported a motion deploring the imminent closure of the museum, calling on the Arts Council for assistance. By April Lord Goodman, Chairman of the Arts Council, had met with the Minister for the Arts and had promised to see if funds could be made available.

No crisis is desirable, but in the story of the Theatre Museum there have been several, each in turn provoking welcome publicity and ultimate solutions. Clouds really can have silver linings. 1967 brought a financial crisis for the British Theatre Museum, and also presented a problem for the author and ballet critic Richard Buckle. An expert on Diaghilev and his circle, Richard Buckle had organised the magnificent Diaghilev Exhibition at the 1954 Edinburgh Festival, assisted by Philip Dyer. In May 1967 Buckle discussed with John Pope-Hennessy, the Director of the Victoria and Albert Museum, the possibility of forming a Diaghilev Collection in the V & A. In September he flew to Paris to see the Diaghilev sets and costumes destined to be sold at Sotheby's in London the following year. The wealth of the material made him determined to save as much as possible, not just for a department of the V & A but for a Museum of the Performing Arts in London. To be more precise, in Covent Garden.

In his book *In The Wake Of Diaghilev*, Richard Buckle relates how he invited John Pope-Hennessy to meet him at his flat overlooking the Covent Garden fruit, vegetable and flower market shortly to be vacated by traders in favour of a more accessible location: 'I told John that I thought the new theatre museum ought to be in Covent Garden for it was the heart of "theatre-land". The first two theatres to be given charters by Charles II after the Commonwealth, when play-acting was forbidden, were Covent Garden and Drury Lane. . . . . What is more, the original "piazza", with its arcades and church in the Tuscan style, had been designed by Inigo Jones, the first great English stage designer.' This meeting was in February 1968.

John Pope-Hennessy was in favour of the idea but regretted that public money for the project was out of the question. Like so many others in this story, Richard Buckle was undeterred. The following April, while cataloguing the costumes for the first Diaghilev sale, Richard Buckle met Lord Goodman, who was already well aware of the problems of the British Theatre Museum Association. Now Mr Buckle made him aware of his discussions with John Pope-Hennessy and the need for public funds to save the Diaghilev material. There were various groups and collections with a single aim. Could they all be brought together? Lord Goodman asked Richard Buckle to write a report on the situation, which he duly presented.

The first Sotheby's sale of Diaghilev material took place on 17 July 1968. Despite the report to Lord Goodman, it was evident that the sale would occur before any possible offer of public funds. The situation seemed hopeless until literally the day of the sale when fate, on cue, intervened. As Richard Buckle was viewing the treasures to be sold that evening, he met Anthony Diamantidi, President of the Diaghilev Foundation selling the material. When Mr Diamantidi heard that Mr Buckle still had no funds, he immediately offered a donation of £25,000 from his own pocket if English backers could raise £75,000. In true dramatic style, with the help of Lord Goodman and a private consortium, a promise of the necessary finance was secured that afternoon, in time for Richard Buckle to bid in the evening. Picasso's monumental and important backcloth for *Le Train Bleu* was purchased for the nation, as well as a Bakst backcloth for *The Sleeping Princess*, and sixty-five costumes.

The story of the Theatre Museum is a story of homeless collections. Just as Committee members of the British Theatre Museum Association stored packets in their cupboards, so the costumes purchased by Mr Buckle found the only accommodation they could in a house in Islington, while the backcloths were stored at the Hayward Gallery. But now there was even more reason for one Theatre Museum to be established. The various collections had grown, and space for storing them was a problem for everyone concerned. John Barber pointed this out in his article 'Dreams of a Living Arts Centre' in the *Daily Telegraph*, August 1969: 'It seems a sad pity that the Enthoven Collection should necessarily be shut away in cupboards and boxes . . . Some idea of how the V & A's collections might be exhibited is to be seen at Leighton House, home of the British Theatre Museum . . . Space, again, is a problem, with no less than nine-tenths of the collection unseen. But before long the BTM must quit its premises, owing to Kensington's future plans for Leighton House. What of course is required is to establish a new and national foundation, a Centre of the Living Arts . . . to create such a centre at Covent Garden following the departure of the Market . . . There could be no more perfect setting, nor a finer memorial in time to come to the greatness of Miss Jennie Lee and the Lords Goodman, Harewood and Norwich.'

A second sale of Diaghilev material took place in December 1969, and again Richard Buckle raised money privately and bought more important costumes and backcloths. There were more objects for the museum, and there were more meetings. Donald Sinden met Lord Goodman and John Pope-Hennessy; they met again with Richard Buckle, and by March 1970 *The Times* was able to report that there was 'further progress on the Museum of Performing Arts front'. At a meeting involving all interested parties, it was decided that the Enthoven Collection at the Victoria and Albert Museum would form the basis of the new museum, which would come under the auspices of the V & A, although in its own home. At the suggestion of John Pope-Hennessy, the committee decided that somebody should be appointed to set up and direct the new venture. At last there was unity, and the lead was being taken by the Victoria and Albert Museum – a Government-funded body. Champagne corks popped.

In 1974 Alexander Schouvaloff was appointed Curator of the Theatre Museum, and an Advisory Council was set up, including as its members Donald Sinden and Richard Buckle. The museum at Leighton House transferred its collections to the Victoria and Albert Museum, and the Fine Rooms at Somerset House were offered as premises for the new museum, due to open in the autumn of 1976. Everyone was delighted that the museum was to become a reality at last, but there were regretful murmurings about a Covent Garden home. The Fine Rooms, simply, were too fine. Theatrical displays needed theatrical lighting, disrespectful to eighteenth-century architecture. Matters rested until a debate occurred the following year about the possible use of the Fine Rooms as a home for paintings by Turner. Moreover, the old Flower Market in Covent Garden had now become vacant. Asked about the relative merits of the two locations, Mr Schouvaloff told a reporter from *The Times* in February 1975: 'The beautiful rooms, with their eighteenth-century painted and stucco ceilings and huge windows, are not the appropriate place for a theatre museum. What is needed is a soundproof dark box to conjure up the magic of the theatre. The Flower Market is the ideal place for the museum.'

April 1975. More newspaper correspondence. More headlines. 'Somerset House for the Turners?'; 'Theatre Museum Controversy in Parliament'; 'Museum: Flower Market Pressure'. The matter was debated in Parliament. In September *The Times* reported the official decision announced by Hugh Jenkins, Minister for the Arts: 'Theatre Museum to be housed in Covent Garden flower market'. Two more years elapsed before the matters could be finalised with the Greater London Council who owned the Flower Market but by August 1977 the opening date of the new museum was announced. 1980 was the year. Mr Schouvaloff and his staff at the V & A celebrated the news with a bottle of champagne.

The next few years saw detailed preparations for the new museum and frustrating delays. Government cut-backs in the arts were reflected in museum budgets and the projected opening date of 1980 was revised to 1982. Even 1982 proved too optimistic: May that year brought instead a Government report on the Science Museum and the Victoria and Albert Museum. Two of its recommendations were shattering. The collections of the Museum of Childhood at Bethnal Green should be closed as an independent outstation of the V & A, while the Theatre Museum project was dismissed as 'a luxury, albeit a delightful one . . .' The author of the report concluded: 'Consideration should be given urgently to abandoning the proposed Theatre Museum at Covent Garden.'

'Preposterous. Myopic. Crazy. Narrow-minded. Short-sighted and retrograde. Wilfully blind. Grotesque.' So began John Barber's article in the *Daily Telegraph*, July 1982, dealing with the conclusions of the Rayner Report. He was not alone in those views, and yet again the letter columns and arts pages of the newspapers were filled with debate on the Theatre Museum. The *Evening Standard* launched a campaign to save the museum and public support was tremendous. The Arts Minister Paul Channon received a petition with 32,000 signatures pleading for the Museum. Following an enquiry by a select committee in the House of Commons, Paul Channon announced in August that the cost of building could be found within the capital programme for the arts. The museum would open in 'about two years'. That news was marvellous.

It seemed too good to be true. It was. In July 1983 it was announced that the Theatre Museum had fallen victim to Government cuts in public expenditure. Roy Strong, Director of the V & A, said that the Theatre Museum as a separate institution would have to be 'suspended till better times', while Richard Buckle remarked: 'My feeling when I heard the news was of despair. It seems that fifteen years' work has gone down the drain.' An article in the *Evening Standard* began: 'If you have tears to shed, prepare to shed them now . . .'

Private munificence had started the collections of the Theatre Museum, and private munificence was now its saviour. New battles were fought in Parliament and in the press. But with the assistance of the Greater London Council and an anonymous donation of £250,000, the war was finally won. On 1 September 1983 a memorandum from The Office of Arts and Libraries announced that the lease on the Flower Market building had been signed and exchanged. The private donation had made it possible for work to start on the conversion of the building in that financial year.

In January 1984 the contractors, Elliotts, started work on the conversion of the Flower Market. On 11 July 1986 they handed over the finished building to Lord Carrington, Chairman of the Board of Trustees of the Victoria and Albert Museum. Over the next nine months the collections and displays were installed in the new premises. Her Royal Highness the Princess Margaret opened the Museum on 23 April 1987, the 423rd anniversary of Shakespeare's birth.

The Shakespeare Industry

Photograph by Graham Brandon

SHAKESPEARE

'I pity the man who cannot enjoy Shakespear.'
George Bernard Shaw

'Whenever an actor comes to him, he should come with hunger and excitement. To make his language work from your brain to your fingertips is to fulfil your profession.'

Laurence Olivier

Mr. WILLIAM
SHAKESPEARES

COMEDIES,
HISTORIES, &
TRAGEDIES.

Publiſhed according to the True Originall Copies.

LONDON
Printed by Iſaac Iaggard, and Ed. Blount. 1623.

Portrait of William Shakespeare (1564–1616)

Published on the title page of the Folio edition of the plays in 1623.

LEAR.   MACBETH.

RICHARD III.ᵈ   HAMLET.

Mʳ GARRICK in Four of his Principal Tragic Characters.

David Garrick (1717–79) in four of his principal tragic characters

Garrick, acknowledged to be the greatest actor ever seen on the English stage, first made his name with his performance as Richard III at Goodman's Fields in 1741. From 1747 until his retirement in 1776 the major part of his career was spent at Drury Lane, where, among other innovations, he introduced new lighting techniques and banished the audience from sitting on the stage itself.

'But when ... I first beheld Garrick, young and light and alive in every muscle and in every feature, heavens, what a transition! It seemed as if a whole century had been stepped over in the transition of a single scene; old things were done away, and a new order at once brought forward, bright and luminous, and clearly destined to dispel the barbarism and bigotry of a tasteless age, too long attached to the prejudices of custom, and superstitiously devoted to the illusions of imposing declamation.'

Richard Cumberland in *Memoirs*, 1806–7

Engraving published c.1770, GE4756

The Theatrical Atlas

A caricature of Edmund Kean (1787–1833) as Richard III supporting the Theatre Royal, Drury Lane. Fire destroyed the theatre on 24 February 1809. Samuel Whitbread, the brewer, raised the necessary £400,000 to rebuild it, and the theatre was reopened on 10 October 1812. The first two seasons lost money, but in 1814 Kean, an obscure provincial actor, began to pack the house and became its great popular star for six years.

Every actor, supported by Shakespeare, has to carry the theatre on his shoulders.

Hand coloured etching, Harry R. Beard Collection CT6924

William Charles Macready (1793–1873) as Macbeth

Macready made his first appearance in Birmingham in 1810. In 1816 he appeared at Covent Garden and by 1819 was established as Edmund Kean's rival at both Covent Garden and Drury Lane. He helped to rescue Shakespeare's original texts from the aberrations performed after the Restoration.

'The greatest – incomparably so – of all living tragedians … His voice – one primary requisite of an actor – is a fine one, powerful, extensive in compass, and containing tones that thrill, and tones that weep. His person is good, and his face very expressive. So that give him a character within his proper range and he will be great in it.'

George Henry Lewes in *The Leader*, 8 February 1851

Hand coloured etching Harry R. Beard Collection, HRB F114–111 CT4028

Playbill for 26 February 1851
Harry R. Beard Collection

Sarah Siddons (1755–1831) as Lady Macbeth at the
Theatre Royal, Drury Lane, 1785

The eldest of Roger Kemble's twelve children, she married the actor William
Siddons when she was 18. Her first appearance with Garrick at Drury Lane in 1775
was a failure but after her return in 1782 she was acclaimed as a great actress.
William Hazlitt said 'She was Tragedy personified.'

'... Since the happy invention of man invested dramatic fiction with seeming
reality, nothing superior, perhaps equal, to the Lady Macbeth of Mrs Siddons has
been seen ... The character of Lady Macbeth became a sort of exclusive possession
to Mrs Siddons. There was a mystery about it which she alone seemed to have
penetrated.'

James Boaden in *Memoirs of Mrs Siddons*, 1827

Engraving
Harry R. Beard Collection

The murder of Lady Macduff in *Macbeth* at the Royal Court Theatre, 1928
Colin Cardew as Macduff's son, Chris Castor as Lady Macduff, Ernest Stidwell and
Douglas Payne as First and Second Murderers.

Top A. Gillette as the Bloody Sergeant, Laurence Olivier as Malcolm, Ivan Brandt as Donalbain and
Cyril Jervis-Walter as Duncan at the Royal Court Theatre, 1928

'I hope we in time shall get audiences to understand Shakespeare so thoroughly that they, too, will take the plays dressed in any kind of costume. Then we can talk about the plays, instead of the way in which we happen to be producing them. "Modern dress" is just a phase we must go through to get rid of the false hair and draperies and an artificial "Shakespearean" technique of acting. Some people think I have adopted it from motives of economy. If they gave it a moment's thought they would know it is not so, because "modern dress", whether man's or woman's, is very much more expensive than fancy dress. Others, again, think I am not sincere about it, and say it is being done merely as a stunt. This is not true. You cannot make a success of anything about which you are not sincere.'

Sir Barry Jackson quoted in *The Times*

Photographs by Lenare

Herbert Beerbohm Tree (1853–1917) as Macbeth

Tree was one of the all-powerful actor managers of the late 19th century and on Irving's death in 1905 he became recognised as leader of the theatrical profession. At Her Majesty's Theatre, which he built in 1897, he maintained the enormously spectacular style of production so popular at the time. Under Tree, the tradition of pictorial realism reached new heights of absurdity and the plays were swamped under vast cumbersome sets and irrelevant detail. However, among Tree's positive achievements were a yearly Shakespeare Festival, at which he revived less popular plays, and the interest he aroused in an audience who might not otherwise have seen or read the plays.

Oil painting by Charles A. Buchel
Harry R. Beard Collection

Edmund Kean as Richard III with John Cooper (1790–1870) as
Richmond

'The excellences and defects of his performance were in general the same
as those which he discovered in Shylock; though, as the character of
Richard is the most difficult, so we think he displayed most power in it
... In one who *dares* so much, there is little indeed to blame.'
　　　William Hazlitt in the *Morning Chronicle*, 15 February 1814.
　Illustrated sheets based on the productions at Covent Garden and
Drury Lane began to be published in 1811. From their price they
became known as 'penny plain' or 'tuppence coloured'. Later, scenes
and texts were published as well as the characters, and toy theatre, or
Juvenile Drama as it was more pompously called, became very popular.
Decorative shapes (particularly of armour) stamped out of sheets of
coloured foil could be stuck onto the paper as an added refinement, as in
the illustration above.

Etching, tinsel and fabric appliqué
Stone Collection CT8432

Right Richard III

Frontispiece engraving from the first illustrated edition of
Shakespeare's works, 1709

Right Henry Irving (1838–1905) as Richard III at the Lyceum Theatre, 1877

Irving became the manager of the Lyceum in 1878 and invited Ellen Terry to join him as his leading lady. Under his management the Lyceum became in all but name the national theatre. Under his leadership the acting profession won a new respectability. Irving refused a knighthood in 1883 but accepted in 1895, the first actor to be knighted.

'I think it has not been your fortune to hear what is called "the house coming down". Even in the epoch of Irving it was seldom that anybody else "brought down the house" – but Irving brought it down . . . You have been to the Russian Ballet perhaps on one of its great nights, or you have heard Chaliapine's reception at Covent Garden. Well, that is not what I mean either. Those are ovations, but mild ovations. The thing I mean had three times the capacity of that.'

Edward Gordon Craig in *Henry Irving*, 1930

Caricature by Alfred Bryan published in *The London Figaro*
Harry R. Beard Collection

Left John Martin Harvey (1863–1944) as Richard III at the Lyceum Theatre, 1910

Martin Harvey joined Irving's Lyceum company in 1882 and remained there for fourteen years. He eventually set up a company under his own management, continuing the traditions of the actor-manager until his death in 1944. His range of productions was wider than that of Irving, and besides Shakespeare he produced and acted in Shaw, Maeterlinck, the poetic dramas of Stephen Phillips and Sophocles. When audiences seemed bewildered by his experiments, he could always reassure them with a revival of *The Only Way*, the immensely successful version of *A Tale of Two Cities* in which he played Sidney Carton.

Photograph by Daily Mirror Studios

Laurence Olivier (b.1907) as Richard III at the New Theatre, 1944

'Olivier's Richard eats into the memory like acid into metal, but the total impression is one of lightness and deftness . . . A lithe performance, black at heart and most astutely mellow in appearance, it is full of baffling, irrational subtleties which will please while they puzzle me as long as I go to theatres.'

Kenneth Tynan in *He That Plays the King*, 1950

Photograph by John Vickers

Queen Katharine: "Lord Cardinal to you I speak" —
Ellen Terry —
Henry VIII.
Stratford: 1902:
Upon-Avon=

THE DUKE, BETWEEN SIR ANDREW AGUE CHEEK AND VIOLA.

Dorothy Jordon (1761–1816) as Viola and others in a scene from *Twelfth Night* at the Theatre Royal, Drury Lane, 1785

Renowned particularly for comedy, she first played at Drury Lane in 1785. During her years at Drury Lane she had four children by Richard Ford who kept promising to marry her, and then in 1791 she became the mistress of the Duke of Clarence (later William IV) by whom she had ten children. She separated from the Duke in 1811 and her last appearance in London was at Covent Garden in 1814.

Hand coloured stipple engraving
Harry R. Beard Collection CT6900

Ellen Terry (1847–1928) as Queen Katharine in *Henry VIII* at Stratford-upon-Avon, 1902

'Ellen Terry was a born actress, and each new piece of work – I would say each performance – was a new birth. Her performances were not made, in the same sense as Irving's were. Her acting was the exact antithesis of his – spontaneous, genial, free . . . With Ellen Terry it was the whole person; even with her head in a bag, she would have captured the house. Tie her hands and ankles, and it would have been harder. So it would seem as though much lay, with her, in her movement – and indeed, an entrance with her, was a gliding, eager thing. She was very rapid in her light, long strides – large in her gestures – measured in her delivery – and impossible to follow in the variety of her expression. She did not depend much on bits of business, as we call them; her power lay in entering any character and making herself one with it – "getting under the skin of a part" is the phrase used by the profession.

And it came to be said of her that she possessed in the very highest degree the art which conceals art. The good actress will ever strive to cover up all traces of how she makes her effects – and the best way to do this is not to make effects, lest the spectator should fancy he is witnessing a display of Brock's fireworks.'
Edward Gordon Craig in *Ellen Terry and Her Secret Self*, 1931

Hand coloured print by Pamela Coleman Smith CT4049

Vivien Leigh (1913–67) as Titania and Robert Helpmann (1909–86) as Oberon in *A Midsummer Night's Dream* at the Old Vic, 1937

Tyrone Guthrie's production was a deliberate pastiche of a 19th-century production of *A Midsummer Night's Dream*. To realise his concept he worked with the greatest of all Romantic designers, Oliver Messel, and as Titania he had the ravishing young Vivien Leigh. Robert Helpmann was at this time the leading dancer with the Vic-Wells Ballet; he asked Lilian Baylis for the chance to play Oberon instead of taking a rise in salary. It was a gamble that paid off for both of them.

Photograph by Gordon Anthony
Courtesy of Radio Times Hulton Picture Library

Donald Calthrop (1888–1940) as Puck in the production by Harley Granville-Barker (1877–1946) of *A Midsummer Night's Dream* at the Savoy Theatre, 1914

Barker showed that there was a way of mounting Shakespeare as an alternative to the elaborate 19th-century productions in which the text was swamped by over-elaborate realistic scenery. His revolutionary production of *A Midsummer Night's Dream* featured golden fairies (literally – they painted their faces with gold leaf) in a setting of a curtained wood. As with most revolutionary productions, everyone complained that the poetry was missing, but the production had a strange, haunting beauty that captivated audiences.

Photograph by Daily Mirror Studios, GH2157

Ralph Richardson (1902–83) as Falstaff and Brian Parker as his page in
Henry IV part 2 at the New Theatre, 1945

'Richardson's Falstaff was not a *comic* performance: it was too rich and many-sided
to be crammed into a single word . . . Richardson never rollicked or slobbered or
staggered: it was not a sweaty fat man, but a dry and dignified one. As the great
belly moved, step following step with great finesse lest it overtopple, the arms
flapped fussily at the sides as if to paddle the body's bulk along. It was deliciously
and subtly funny, not riotously so: from his height of pomp Falstaff was chuckling
at himself: it was not we alone, laughing at him.'

Kenneth Tynan in *He That Plays the King*, 1950

Photograph by John Vickers

Ellen Terry as Juliet in *Romeo and Juliet*, which she first played at the Lyceum Theatre in 1882

Juliet was not one of Ellen Terry's most admired roles, and she herself was not pleased with her performance: 'Perhaps I was neither young enough nor old enough to play Juliet ... Now I understand Juliet better. Now I know how she should be played ... But time is inexorable. At sixty, know what one may, one cannot play Juliet ... I did not *look* right. My little daughter Edy, a born archaeologist, said "Mother, you oughtn't to have a fringe." Yet, strangely enough, Henry [Irving] himself liked me as Juliet.'

Ellen Terry in *The Story of My Life*

Photograph by Window and Grove
Guy Little Collection GK4534

Eliza O'Neill (1791–1827) as Juliet, at Covent Garden, c.1815

Hand coloured mezzotint
Harry R. Beard Collection CT4047

26

MISS FANNY KEMBLE as JULIET.

Pub. by J. & M. SMEE, H. Swan S.ᵗ Minories London.

Fanny Kemble (1809–93) as Juliet at Covent Garden, 1829

One of the famous theatrical family, she was the daughter of Charles (1775–1854). Her three years at Covent Garden under her father's management were so successful that they saved the theatre from bankruptcy. In 1832 she went to America and in 1834 married Pierce Butler from Philadelphia but the marriage was an unhappy one. She divorced her husband in 1845 and then began to give a series of popular readings. Her last appearance, in a reading, was in New York City in 1868.

'To those who really love Shakespeare, and have any feeling for what is highest in dramatic art, there can be no performance half so fascinating as these readings. By means of changes of voice, unforced yet marked, and sufficient gesticulation to explain the text, aided by the fine commentary of eye and brow, Mrs Kemble brings before you the whole scene, enacts every part, and moves you as the play itself would move you.'
George Henry Lewes, 'Mrs Kemble's Shakespeare Readings' in *The Leader*, 29 March 1851

Hand coloured etching
Harry R. Beard Collection CT3794

left
Considered to be a worthy successor of Sarah Siddons, Eliza O'Neill's first appearance as Juliet was a triumph. Her early retirement in 1819 to marry Mr (later Sir William) Becher was a great disappointment for her public.

'The stage has lost one of its principal ornaments and fairest supports, in the person of Miss O'Neill . . . Her excellence (unrivalled by any actress since Mrs Siddons) consisted in truth of nature and force of passion. Her correctness did not seem the effect of art or study, but of instinctive sympathy, of a conformity of mind and disposition to the character she was playing, as if she had unconsciously become the very person. There were no catching lights, no pointed hits, no theatrical tricks, no female arts resorted to, in her best or general style of acting; there was a singleness, an entireness, and harmony in it, that gave it a double charm as well as a double power.'
William Hazlitt on 'Miss O'Neill's retirement' in *London Magazine*, February 1820

Henry Irving (1838–1905)
as Shylock at the Lyceum
Theatre, 1879

Laurence Olivier as Shylock, National Theatre Company at the Old Vic, 1970

Olivier played Shylock in a production with a late 19th-century setting directed by Jonathan Miller.

'He wore a . . . Disraeli-style curl on his forehead; the not-quite-immaculate cut of his striped trousers and the affected dropping of his final g's gave subtle evidence of the pseudo upper-class gentility of this frock-coated Jew; and the slightly protruding upper teeth that showed when he smiled was another touch neatly designed to give the man an unsavoury visual image.'

John Cottrell, *Laurence Olivier*, 1975

Photograph by Anthony Crickmay

Irving's portrayal of Shylock as a gentle, misunderstood, noble Jew was challenged as being Irving before Shakespeare, but it was a good example of his power.

'. . . though his reading of a character might be challenged, it could never be forgotten: you might be unable wholeheartedly to accept . . . Irving as Shylock, but you nevertheless saw Shylock as Irving for the rest of your life.'

W. Graham Robertson in *Time Was*, 1931

His Shylock costume was never replaced and only once cleaned in its stage life.

Photograph by Lock & Whitfield, GE6373

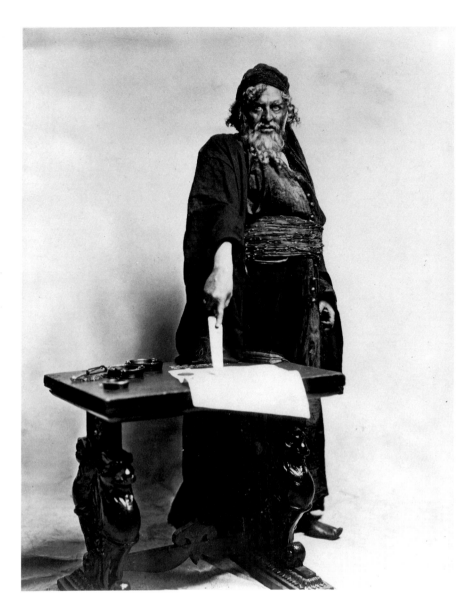

Herbert Beerbohm Tree as Shylock at Her Majesty's Theatre, 1908

'. . . an abundantly racial portrait in oils of an inflexible enemy, a man accompanied always by the repulsive figure of Tubal . . . All of it was hysterically theatrical; and Tree kept it up until the Trial scene when Shylock at last was granted the real authority he had needed earlier. Such a man as this would never have borne enforced conversion; at the sentence Shylock fainted in Tubal's arms.'

J.C. Trewin in *Shakespeare on the English Stage 1900–1964*, 1964

Photograph by F.W. Burford, N697

Edmund Kean as Shylock

Kean made his fortune through Richard III, but he established his reputation as Shylock, which he performed at Drury Lane for the first time in 1814.

'Mr Kean last night made his appearance at Drury Lane Theatre in the character of Shylock. For voice, eye, action, and expression, no actor has come out for many years at all equal to him. The applause, from the first scene to the last, was general, loud and uninterrupted. Indeed, the very first scene in which he comes on with Bassanio and Antonio, showed the master in his art, and at once decided the opinion of the audience.'

William Hazlitt on 'Mr Kean's Shylock' in the *Morning Chronicle*, 27 January 1814

Hand coloured mezzotint
Harry R. Beard Collection CT4356B

Edmund Kean as Othello

'We, who remember Kean in *Othello*, may surely be excused if we believe that we have seen Othello *acted*, and so acted as there is little chance of our seeing it acted again.'

George Henry Lewes from *On Actors and the Art of Acting*

Hand coloured lithograph
Given by Miss Callwell, CT9395

Playbill for 25 March 1833

Inscribed: 'The last time Kean appeared in public – he was taken ill in the middle of the play and Mr Warde finished the piece, he never played again. "Othello's occupation's gone".'

Harry R. Beard Collection

IRA ALDRIDGE ALS OTHELLO.

Ira Aldridge (1804–67) as Othello, 1855

This American negro actor is thought to have been Kean's servant during his first tour of America. Kean brought him back to England and encouraged him in his acting career. Aldridge first appeared in London as Othello at the Royalty Theatre in 1826. He was especially popular in Germany where he acted in English while his supporting cast spoke in German.

Lithograph inscribed and signed by Aldridge and dated 26 August 1855
N696

right
'... a kind of bad acting of which only a great actor is capable ... Alone so far among critics, perhaps alone forever among audiences, I find Sir Laurence Olivier's Othello the most prodigious and perverse example of this in a decade.'
Alan Brien in the *Sunday Telegraph*

Laurence Olivier as Othello, National Theatre Company at the Old Vic, 1964

Photograph by Angus McBean

Charles Young (1777–1856) as Hamlet and Julia Glover (1779–1850) as Ophelia at the Theatre Royal, Haymarket, 1807

Young's first appearance in London was as Hamlet in 1807, when 'he was most rapturously received'. He was one of the finest disciples of the formal, classical style of acting as exemplified by John Philip Kemble. Julia Glover (née Betterton – she was said to be descended from the great Restoration actor Thomas Betterton), first appeared at Covent Garden in 1797. Described by Macready as 'a rare thinking actress', she was one of the first women to play Hamlet. She chose the role for her benefit performance in 1832 and won the admiration of Edmund Kean for her portrayal.

Oil painting by George Clint
Victoria and Albert Museum, Dyce Collection

Edward Gordon Craig (1872–1966) as Hamlet, which he first performed in
Hereford, 1894

'The joy of acting Hamlet on Tuesday was almost inconceivable to anybody except
a young man who, knowing the lines, goes on and hopes for the best. Because, say
what you may – and you may even think it without saying it – to play Hamlet and
to play Romeo is, after all, very difficult, and if we knew how difficult it was we
shouldn't go on at all.'

Edward Gordon Craig from Index to the Story of my Days

Oil painting by William Rothenstein
Given by Sir John Rothenstein

Albert Finney (b.1936) in rehearsal for *Hamlet*,
National Theatre at the Old Vic, 1975

'Finney presents us, in fact, not with a romantic princeling or a contemporary weakling but a Renaissance student whose passion is constantly at odds with the "sovereignty of reason" ... It is a thrilling active disturbing performance compact with humour and grace; and it is sans question the best Hamlet since Redgrave's.'

Michael Billington in the *Guardian*, 12 December 1975

Photograph by Anthony Crickmay

Sarah Bernhardt (1845–1923) as Hamlet at the Théâtre Sarah Bernhardt,
Paris, 1899

'I believe her to have been guided by an infallible instinct, and whatever she said or
whatever she did, she could not go wrong. It is impossible to analyse and define the
effect of genius, but in the case of Sarah Bernhardt, there are three main factors:
gesture and gait, voice, and facial expression. Nobody ever moved better . . . Then
there was her voice, that languishing voice, so soft, so melting, so perfectly in tune
and in time, with so sure a rhythm, and so perfectly clean-cut that one never lost a
syllable, even when the words seemed to float from her like a sigh . . . Then there
was her facial expression. No actress or actor ever made greater play with the eyes:
now wistful and wondering, now like "magic casements" opening on all that was
most far away and most forlorn; now like glinting gems, hard as metal and cold as
ice, and now like darts of flame, piercing you with their pointed brilliance; now
blazing with fury or flooded with passion; now sad with all the sorrows of the
world . . .'

Maurice Baring in Sarah Bernhardt, 1933

Photograph by Lafayette GE6377

Henry Irving as Hamlet
at the Lyceum Theatre, 1874

'There are not many audiences which will re-
linquish their beer for the sake of art. This
was a very special occasion. But the supreme
moment for the audience had come when the
curtain fell. If they had sacrificed their refresh-
ment, waiting there, as many of them had
done, since three o'clock in the afternoon,
they had done something for art. They had, at
least, deserved the pleasure of cheering the
artist who had inspired them. It was no *succès
d'estime*. The actor of the evening had, in the
teeth of tradition, in the most unselfish manner, and in the most highly artistic fashion,
convinced his hearers that William Hazlitt,
the critic, was right. Here was the Hamlet
who thinks aloud; here was the scholar, and
so little of the actor. So they threw crowns,
and wreaths and bouquets, at the artist, and
the good people felt that this artistic assistance had come at a turning point in the history of English dramatic art.'

Clement Scott
in *From 'The Bells' to 'King Arthur'*, 1896

Wood engraving
GG1959

Johnston Forbes-Robertson (1853–1937) as
Hamlet at the Lyceum Theatre, 1897

'Mr Forbes-Robertson is essentially a classical
actor ... What I mean by classical is that he
can present a dramatic hero as a man whose
passions are those which have produced the
philosophy, the poetry, the art, and the state-
craft of the world, and not merely those which
have produced its weddings, coroners' in-
quests, and executions. And that is just the
sort of actor that *Hamlet* requires.'

George Bernard Shaw, 'Hamlet', 2 October
1897, from *Our Theatres in the Nineties*

Photograph by Lizzie Caswall Smith
Harry R. Beard Collection

To Gabrielle - my love and affectionate good wishes always. John - 'Hamlet' 1934.

John Gielgud (b.1904) as Hamlet at the New Theatre, 1934

'Many times people have asked me if I saw Forbes-Robertson, and have then gone on to say, was he better than Gielgud? The answer is "For me – no"; but I do not give it with entire confidence. I saw Forbes-Robertson when I was young and inexperienced and he was elderly; I saw Gielgud when I was mature and experienced and he was young. How can a fair comparison be made when conditions are so unequal? Only, I think, in one way; Forbes-Robertson left no detailed impression on my memory ...

Quite different is the effect left upon my mind by John Gielgud's first Hamlet, at the Old Vic in 1929. Here too the memory of exquisite speaking – the music not so grand because the voice, considered simply as an instrument, is less impressive. But in Gielgud's speaking of the verse there was that extraordinary quality which was not matched in Forbes-Robertson's – the sense of immediacy, as if the words were coming straight from the speaker's brain. I remember listening with delight while passage after passage, so familiar to me that I could almost have delivered them myself, came to my ear as if new-coined that moment. Time and again I said to myself, "I don't believe I ever took that phrase in fully till now." The secret lay, of course, in the actor's utter concentration on the meaning of the words he was speaking, rather than their sound. His mind was at full stretch in a way and to a degree that players trained in the more declamatory methods of the actor's theatre had not found necessary; and so he was able to keep the minds of his audiences at full stretch too.'

W.A. Darlington in *Six Thousand and One Nights*, 1960

Photograph by Yvonne Gregory
Given by Sir John Gielgud HC2713

John Gielgud as Benedick at the Shakespeare Memorial Theatre,
Stratford-upon-Avon, 1950

David Garrick as Benedick, c.1770

'Though Mr Garrick's merit in Tragedy is very apparent, we are nevertheless inclined to think that Comedy is his more particular *fort.* . . . In Benedic [sic] he has given us the highest specimen of the sprightly and the Humorous.'

From *The Theatrical Review or Annals of the Drama*, 1763

Watercolour and gold paint on vellum by Jean-Louis Fesch (1738–73)

'. . . I kept trying to make Benedick into more of a soldier. At first Mariano [Andreu, the designer] encouraged me to be a dandy, wearing comic hats, one like a blancmange, another with a round brim trimmed with feathers. The hats used to get laughs the moment I came on in them. I decided that this had not much to do with Shakespeare's play, so I gradually became less of the courtier. . . . Benedick ought to be an uncouth soldier, a tough misanthrope, who wears a beard and probably smells to high heaven. When this went against the grain I tried to console myself with the idea that Irving must have been more of the courtier too . . .'

John Gielgud in *An Actor and his Time*, 1979

Queen Victoria at the Royal Opera House, Covent Garden, 19 April 1855

Throughout her life, Queen Victoria was very interested in the theatre. In her youth she often went to the opera and ballet and her delightful drawings of the dancers and singers she saw (which are in the Royal Library at Windsor) give a very accurate impression of the performances. Later, she had regular 'command' performances at Windsor and at Buckingham Palace.

'The visit of Her Majesty had been expected. The opera house was filled in every part to overflowing; and on the entrance of the Queen the expression of enthusiasm was electrical. The whole audience rose to its feet, and one loud deep burst of congratulatory applause burst forth from the vast concourse of human beings. Hats and handkerchiefs were waved. Many ladies sobbed aloud. During this demonstration the Queen stood at the front of her box and curtsied repeatedly, while Prince Albert bowed in reply to the deafening congratulations. The audience would not allow the opera to proceed till the *National Anthem* had been sung, and, as a mark of respect, Lablache and Persiani joined the rest of the company. At the words "Scatter her enemies", in particular, the most deafening acclamations arose, and one cheer more was raised when Her Majesty resumed her seat in the corner of the box.'

Benjamin Lumley in *Reminiscences of the Opera*, 1864,
describing the visit to Her Majesty's Theatre on 31 May 1842

Hand coloured mezzotint
Harry R. Beard Collection HRB F125–60 CT5117

OPERA

Sold by R: Bremner in the Strand LONDON.

'Opera is perhaps the most elaborate of art forms ... It offers to its creators a breadth of resource unknown to most other art forms, not only because of its appeal to many susceptibilities but also because music can strengthen, subtilise or inflect any words that are uttered on the stage. It can also carry hints about words or feelings that are left unexpressed.'

Stanley Sadie

'A civilised country must have a great and good quality opera house.'

Lord Goodman

Madame CATALANI in SEMIRAMIDE,
her first Appearance in England, Dec' 13th, 1806.

Angelica Catalani (1780–1849) in the title role of Portogallo's *Semiramide* at the
King's Theatre, 1806

Angelica Catalani made her first appearance on the London stage in this role. She also gave the first performance in England, in 1812, of Susanna in Mozart's *The Marriage of Figaro*, and became one of the highest-paid singers on the operatic stage, receiving two hundred guineas for singing *God Save The King* and *Rule Britannia*.

'On the latter occasion (22 April 1825), she sang Rode's variation "God save the King", and "Rule Britannia". At the end of the last song, which was loudly encored, she made her obeisance to every part of the audience, and retired amidst universal applause, waving of handkerchiefs by the ladies, and continual cries of bravi. Catalani, who frequently used to say that she could get more money by singing in an English barn than in a continental palace, found these concerts very profitable.'

W.T. Parke in *Musical Memoirs*, 1830

Hand coloured lithograph
Harry R. Beard Collection HRB F103–21

Costume de M.lle SONTAG, rôle de ROSINE,
dans le Barbier de Séville.

Th. Royal Italien.

Opéra.

N.º 640.

Maleuvre S.

Chez Hautecœur Martinet, Libraire, rue du Coq N.º 13 et 15. à Paris.

Henriette Sontag (1806–54) as Rosina in Rossini's *Il Barbieri di Siviglia* at the King's Theatre, 1828

'The voice of Mademoiselle Sontag is a soprano: it is full, clear, and sweet, and her taste is very highly cultivated. In the cavatina, 'Una voce poco fa', she introduced two staccato passages, which she executed with surprising rapidity and neatness of articulation; and in the music lesson of the second act she sang Rodes' variations, particularly that in the arpeggios, in a style superior to Catalani. At the close of the opera she was loudly called for, when she came forward again, and was greeted with acclamation.'

W.T. Parke in *Musical Memoirs*, 1830

Hand coloured etching
Harry R. Beard Collection

Geo. B. Rubini.

Giovanni Battista Rubini (1794–1854) as Arturo Talbo in Bellini's *I Puritani*

Rubini was the Italian tenor who created the role of Talbo in the first Paris production in 1835. Bellini also composed the tenor parts in *Il Pirata* and *La Sonnambula* for him. Rubini, with his rich and powerful voice, was a sensational success in London between 1831 and 1842.

'The next great event, and one which brought my first season (1842) through all its difficulties and dangers to a successful conclusion, was the re-appearance of the great tenor Rubini. He was announced for a limited number of nights only, previous to his final retirement from the stage. The intense desire to hear the last notes of this long-established favourite of the frequenters of the opera, brought crowded houses, during every one of his performances, which commenced on the 13th of June, until the end of the season. In the *Sonnambula*, in *Don Giovanni*, in the *Puritani*, in the *Matrimonio Segreto*, and in *Anna Bolena*, in *Otello*, in *Così Fan Tutti*, and in his favourite air from the *Pirata* (given on the nights when he did not appear in a whole opera), sung with an embroidery as delicate as Mechlin lace – in all these parts he was listened to with rapture, up to his final farewell . . .

Never probably was there another singer who so absolutely commanded the admiration of his brother artists. I remember well that in the "good old times", when he was executing one of his fascinating arias, Lablache and others of "the corps" would linger at the wings, as though unwilling to lose one of his enchanting notes. Considering how unusual it is for one singer to take much interest in the performance of another, this fact is significant of Rubini's power of enchaining the ear of his listeners.'

Benjamin Lumley in *Reminiscences of the Opera*, 1864

Hand coloured lithograph by Alfred Edward Chalon RA
Harry R. Beard Collection CT3751

46

Antonio Tamburini (1800–76) as Riccardo in Bellini's *I Puritani*

This Italian baritone created the role of Riccardo in Paris in 1835. He appeared regularly in London from 1832 at His Majesty's Theatre, where he was idolised by audiences. In 1840 the manager refused to engage him for the season and the 'Tamburini row' erupted, culminating in nightly demonstrations by the audience. The management gave in. By 1847, Tamburini was in an exceptionally strong company engaged for Covent Garden, so beginning that theatre's reputation as a leading opera house, as opposed to a theatre where opera was occasionally presented.

Hand coloured lithograph by Alfred Edward Chalon RA
Harry R. Beard Collection
CT3750

Luigi Lablache (1794–1858) as Dulcamara in Donizetti's *L'Elisir d'Amore*

An Italian bass of French and Irish parentage, Lablache was a huge man. He sang regularly in London from 1830 to 1856. He remained loyal to Her Majesty's Theatre at the time of Tamburini's row but sang at Covent Garden from 1854. For a short time he gave singing lessons to Queen Victoria.

'Lablache's voice is an organ of most extraordinary power. It is impossible by description to give any notion of its volume of sound ... One may have some idea of this power of tone when it can truly be asserted that, the entire opera band and chorus playing and singing *forte*, his voice may be as distinctly heard as a trumpet among violins. He is the very stentor of vocalists. When he sings he rouses the audience as the bugle does the warhorse, or as the songs of Tyrtaeus reanimated the Spartans. With this prodigious vehicle of sound, his singing is distinguished by superior softness and expression. He is a great master of his art, and manages the lights and shades with judgment and skill.'

Lord Mount-Edgcumbe quoted by Benjamin Lumley in *Reminiscences of the Opera*, 1864

Hand coloured etching
Harry R. Beard Collection L3

The soprano known as the 'Swedish nightingale' for the purity of her voice, Lind studied with Manuel Garcia and made her debut as Norma in 1844. After one of her performances as Amina in Vienna the Empress was so impressed that she threw her a bouquet onto the stage – an unprecedented action. In 1847 Lind was engaged to appear at Her Majesty's Theatre as the rival attraction to those singers who had gone to Covent Garden. After 1849 she only sang in concerts and oratorios. She died in Malvern.

'In the part of Amina, in *La Sonnambula*, she surpassed all previous expectations. In simplicity, tenderness, and grace, in perfect impersonation, these qualities being combined with exquisite delivery of the music, she was universally declared to have beaten all her compeers "out of the field". Not only was she *the Sonnambula*, but Amina was generally looked upon as the culminating point of her unprecedently successful season.'

Benjamin Lumley in *Reminiscences of the Opera*, 1864

Hand coloured lithograph
Harry R. Beard Collection L42

Mad.lle Jenny Lind, as Amina, in La Sonnambula.

Jenny Lind (1820–87) as Amina in Bellini's *La Sonnambula*

Fanny Persiani (1812–67) as Zerlina in Mozart's *Don Giovanni*

An Italian soprano who sang in London from 1835 to 1849. Her voice, described as clear and penetrating, was much admired by connoisseurs. It was Persiani's husband who, with others, purchased the lease of the Royal Italian Opera House in 1847. The prospectus for the first season of their new company announced that it had been established: 'for the purpose of rendering a more perfect performance of the lyric drama than has hitherto been attained in this country.' From this date Covent Garden's position as the leading opera house was established.

Hand coloured lithograph
Harry R. Beard Collection
HRB F8–10 CT4042

Giuditta Pasta (1797–1865) in the title role of
Bellini's *Norma*

Italian soprano, an almost legendary figure renowned for her dramatic interpretations, Pasta created
Donizetti's Anna Bolena (1830) and Bellini's Amina (1831), Norma (1831) and Beatrice di Tenda (1833).
She frequently appeared in London from 1824 until 1837 and first sang the part of Norma in 1833. In 1850
she tried to make a comeback but her voice had gone.

Watercolour caricature by Alfred Edward Chalon RA, 1833
Department of Prints and Drawings
E3328–1922 CT5358

LEOPOLD MOZART, *Pere de* MARIANNE MOZART, *Virtuose âgée de onze ans et de* J. G. WOLFGANG MOZART, *Compositeur et Maitre de Musique âgé de sept ans.*

Wolfgang Amadeus Mozart (1756–91) aged 7, with his father Leopold (1719–87), and his sister Marianne

Lithograph after a drawing made in 1764
Harry R. Beard Collection
M119

Pauline Lucca (1841–1908) as Cherubino in Mozart's *Le Nozze di Figaro*

An Austrian soprano with a vocal range of two and a half octaves, Pauline Lucca made her London debut at Covent Garden in 1863. She became a great favourite, appearing almost every season until 1872. She was especially admired in dramatic roles, and her Cherubino and Carmen were considered to be unsurpassed in their day.

Photograph by Disderi
Guy Little Collection CH3855

Nellie Melba (1859–1931) as Juliette in
Gounod's *Roméo et Juliette*

Melba was an Australian soprano who, as well
as having an ice-cream sundae and a special
kind of toast named after her, had her first huge
success as Juliette at Covent Garden in 1889.
As *prima donna assoluta* she appeared there until
1914 (except 1909) and again after the war until
1924. She reigned supreme, brooking no rivals,
and possibly influencing casting. A high
coloratura of exceptional range, her voice re-
tained its great freshness and purity to the end,
and the insolent ease of her technique and brilliant ornamentation were greatly admired. Her
acting, however, was restricted, and many
found her a cold performer.

Photograph by Dupont
GH3862

Right
The first public performance of this Italian soprano was at a concert in 1850. Her fame dates
from her interpretation of Amina at Covent
Garden in 1861 and she appeared there for 25
consecutive seasons. She became the most
highly paid singer of her day at 200 guineas per
performance and her contract also stipulated
that she did not have to attend rehearsals. After
her second marriage she lived for many years at
Craig-y-Nos Castle in Wales, where she built
her own private theatre.

Photograph by C. Silvy
Guy Little Collection
GH3827

Adelina Patti (1843–1919) as Amina in
Bellini's *La Sonnambula*

Photograph by C. Silvy
Guy Little Collection
GH3828

Adelina Patti as Catherine in Meyerbeer's
L'Etoile du Nord

Francesco Tamagno (1850–1905) in the title role and Antonio Scotti (1866 – 1936) as Iago in Verdi's *Otello* at the Royal Opera House, Covent Garden, 1901

Edouard de Reszke (1855–1917) as Méphistophélès in Gounod's *Faust*

One of the greatest basses of all time. His first appearance was as the King of Egypt in the Paris premiere of *Aida* in 1876, conducted by Verdi. He possessed an imposing stage presence and a powerful dramatic personality, allied to a bass voice of great power and richness, yet, unusually, he was able to encompass rapid passages with great ease. He made the role of Mephistopheles particularly his own, and sang it in the 500th performance of *Faust* at the Paris Opéra in 1887. He left the stage in 1903 and retired to his estates in Poland, where he died in poverty. His brother, Jean de Reszke (1850–1925), was an equally great tenor.

Photograph by Mieczkowski
GH3861

Top
Tamagno was the greatest *tenor di forza* in the history of opera. He created the role of Otello at La Scala, Milan in 1887 and gave the first performance in London in 1889. Some of his other great parts were Ernani, Don Carlos, Radamès in *Aida*, Adorno in the revised version of *Simon Boccanegra*. His final appearances were in 1904.
Scotti was a fine baritone and an outstanding actor. He gave the first performance of Scarpia in Puccini's *Tosca* in London in 1900.
Drawing by Allan Stewart reproduced in *The Illustrated London News*, 29 June 1901. (The original drawing is in the Theatre Museum)

Harry R. Beard Collection V93

Feodor Chaliapine (1873–1938) in the title role of Mussorgsky's *Boris Godunov*,
in the coronation scene

'The first presentation of Modeste Mussorgsky's *Boris Godunov* (at the Theatre
Royal, Drury Lane, 1913) could only be described as a great artistic explosion . . .
The focal point of this wonderful explosion was Chaliapin himself who headed the
company. He was a man of the people, and it was something he never forgot . . .'
James Hanley, Introduction to
Chaliapin, an Autobiography as told to Maxim Gorky, 1968

Chaliapine's coronation scene costume is in the Museum's collection

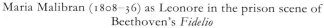

Maria Malibran (1808–36) as Leonore in the prison scene of
Beethoven's *Fidelio*

Maria Malibran came from a distinguished family of singers
and teachers of singing of Spanish origin, her father being the
great Manuel Garcia. A mezzo-soprano, she first appeared in
England in 1825 at the King's Theatre, and quickly established
herself as a popular favourite, hailed for her passionate performances. So great was her drawing-power that, when she
moved to Covent Garden, the management arranged mar-
athon opera evenings in 1833 when *The Marriage of Figaro*
would be followed by *Fidelio*, or *La Sonnambula* (in which
Malibran sang Susanna) by *Der Freischütz*. She died in
Manchester at the early age of 28, as a result of a riding
accident.

Hand coloured lithograph
Harry R. Beard Collection F132–10
CT4036A

Flagstad, a Norwegian soprano, made her debut in 1913. For twenty years she sang only in Scandinavia in opera and operetta, but in 1933, when she was on the verge of retiring, she accepted an engagement to sing small roles at Bayreuth. By the time of her debut at the Metropolitan Opera in New York two years later, she was hailed as the greatest Wagnerian soprano of the day. She first appeared at Covent Garden in 1936, and after the war she returned and did much to help re-establish the Wagner repertory there.

Kirsten Flagstad (1895–1962) as Brunnhilde in *Die Walküre*, Royal Opera House, Covent Garden, 1936

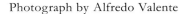

Photograph by Alfredo Valente

Hans Hotter (b.1909) as Wotan in Wagner's *Der Ring des Nibelungen* at the Royal Opera House, Covent Garden, c.1960

A German bass-baritone, Hotter first appeared at Covent Garden in 1947 and performed regularly until 1967, establishing himself as the leading Wotan in both London and Bayreuth.

'No other Wotan seemed to be able to stretch his spear-bearing arm to such godlike length, and it was essentially the size of the impersonation, dramatic as well as vocal, matching the gigantic figure of the King of the Gods, that put Hotter on a pedestal amongst the Wotans of his generation.'

Lord Harewood
in *The Tongs and the Bones*, 1981

Elisabeth Schwarzkopf (b.1915) as the Princess of Werdenberg (the Marschallin)
and Kurt Böhme (b.1908) as Baron Ochs in Richard Strauss' *Der Rosenkavalier*
at the Royal Opera House, Covent Garden, 1959

Schwarzkopf, a German soprano, made her debut in Berlin in 1938. She sang
regularly in London from 1947. Exquisite in Mozart and an outstanding Marschallin, she also created Anne Trulove in Stravinsky's *The Rake's Progress*. Her
farewell performance was in Brussels in 1972 as the Marschallin.

Böhme, German bass-baritone, made his debut in 1930 in Dresden where he stayed
until 1950. He appeared in London regularly between 1956 and 1970.

Photograph by Houston Rogers

Joan Sutherland (b.1926) as Lucia in Donizetti's *Lucia di Lammermoor* at the
Royal Opera House, Covent Garden, 1959

Australian soprano, and one of the world's leading dramatic coloraturas, Sutherland established herself with particular success in the Bellini and Donizetti repertory. She made her debut in London at Covent Garden in 1952, and created a sensation with her performance of Lucia in 1959. Since then she has sung all over the world, in every leading opera house, and she sang in the first performances at the Sydney Opera House in 1974. Her husband, Richard Bonynge (b.1930), conducts most of her performances.

Photograph by Houston Rogers

Maria Callas (1923–77) in the title role of Puccini's *Tosca* at the Royal Opera House, Covent Garden

The greatest dramatic soprano of her time. She made her debut in 1938 and was at her peak between 1951 and 1964.

'Her range of musical interests was limited but her musical ambition boundless; she raised vocal display to a quite new level of expression for our times and yet had a vocal method that was never quite secure. She would occasionally refer to, and indeed treat, her own voice as if it were a force belonging to her but somehow outside her; as if it were waiting with some reluctance to do her bidding as it had before, but always essentially a force to be tamed.'

Lord Harewood in *The Tongs and the Bones*, 1981

Photograph by Houston Rogers

Tito Gobbi (1913–84) as Scarpia in Puccini's *Tosca* at the Royal Opera House,
Covent Garden, 1964

This Italian baritone's musicianship and intelligence made him one of the finest
singers of his generation, with a repertory of nearly one hundred operas. He made
his debut in 1935 while still a student. His Covent Garden debut was in 1950, and
he appeared there regularly for the remainder of his career. It was here that his
interpretation of Scarpia reached its peak, in a series of legendary performances
opposite Maria Callas, in 1964. As the size of his repertory implies, Gobbi's range
of characterisation was extraordinary. His mastery of make-up was no less so. For
each role he devised the exact make-up that gave physical form to the character – in
performance could be seen how subtle was Gobbi's blending of the physical form
and the interpretation of the role.

Photograph by Houston Rogers

Sir Arthur Seymour Sullivan (1842–1900)

With Gilbert as librettist, Sullivan wrote 14 operas and many of his tunes have entered the subconscious minds of most English people. Without Gilbert he was more concerned with writing 'serious' music which received less popular acclaim. Caricature by Ape [Carlo Pellegrini (1838–89)] published in *Vanity Fair*

Colour lithograph CT4946

Sir William Schwenck Gilbert (1836–1911)

An irascible but brilliantly clever satirist, dramatist and rhymer, he consistently provided Sullivan with ingenious words to stretch the composer's capacity for writing a memorable tune.
Caricature by Spy [Leslie Ward (1851–1922)] published in *Vanity Fair*

Colour lithograph CT4945

Programme cover for the Savoy Theatre, 17 October 1881

CT4951

Clara Dow (1886–1969) as Phyllis in *Iolanthe* at the Savoy Theatre, 1907

The D'Oyly Carte Opera Company

Poster designed by Dudley Hardy for the first revival of *The Yeomen of the Guard* at the Savoy Theatre, 1897.

Colour lithograph   Ent 1881 CT4372

Henry Lytton (1865–1936) as Bunthorne in *Patience*, at the Savoy Theatre, 1901

'Lytton's acting always seems to be in such perfect "poise". It is so refined and spontaneous. Each point receives its full measure, and yet is so free of exaggeration of "clowning". He is, that is to say, an artiste to his finger-tips, and no real artiste, even when he is a humorist, has any place for buffoonery. Like the Gilbert and Sullivan operas themselves, he is always so clean and wholesome and pleasant. The clearness of his enunciation is a gift in itself, and his dancing reminds us of the time when all our dancing was so charming and graceful.'

From the Introduction to *The Secrets of a Savoyard* by Henry A. Lytton, 1922

Watercolour, inscribed by W.S. Gilbert

Left

Always appreciative of an attractive soprano, it was W.S. Gilbert himself who picked Clara Dow from the chorus line to play the part of Elsie in the revival of *The Yeomen of the Guard* at the Savoy Theatre in 1907. She played principal roles with the D'Oyly Carte Company for the next seven years.

'A striking example of the acquisition of the Gilbertian spirit is found in Miss Clara Dow who, as Phyllis, is altogether charming. She has the naive style the part demands, and sings the music with much grace and vocal beauty.'

Contemporary critic

Photograph
HB3186

He Danc'd like a Monkey, his Pockets will cram'd;
Caper'd off with a Grin. Kiss my A—— & be D——d.

Pub.d Jan.y 10.th 1781. by W. Humphrey N.o 227, Strand.

Auguste Vestris (1760–1842)

A member of the famous family of Italian dancers and, by all accounts, a greater dancer than his father, Gaetano. He made his debut at the Paris Opéra in 1772 and was *premier danseur* there for 36 years. In 1781 he appeared in London with his father. They were both pelted with orange peel because the price of the seats had been raised but at the end of the performance they were ecstatically applauded. His fee for the performance was £600 and this illustration, based on a 'straight' drawing of Vestris, satirises his alleged rapaciousness. In 1791 he was ballet-master at the King's Theatre. His last appearance was at the age of 75 with Taglioni, who was then 31.

Etching and aquatint
Given by Dame Marie Rambert from the Marie Rambert-Ashley Dukes Collection
E 4966–1968 CT8304

BALLET

'Dancing consists of nothing more than the art of displaying elegant and precise shapes in different positions favourable to the development of lines . . . It is essentially pagan, materialistic and sensual.'

Théophile Gautier

'New audiences for ballet, of course, are not created by new dances that have just a passing interest. What makes an audience, what makes a newcomer committed is a dance that will cause him to ask, "When can I see that *again*?" Those are the ballets we are all looking for.'

George Balanchine

Marie Taglioni (1804–84) in *La Sylphide*

This ballet, with choreography by Filippo Taglioni (1778–1871), Marie's father, was performed for the first time in Paris in 1832. It embodied Romantic ideals and changed the course of ballet. Marie Taglioni was the first to wear what became the conventional ballet costume and she established dancing on point as part of the dancer's normal technique. After *La Sylphide* she became a world-famous star and few other dancers have had such an international reputation.

'With *La Sylphide* a new spirit invades the scene, glides over the stage, soars towards the "flies". No revolution in the order of ideas could have been more complete. Fairy-tale takes the place of mythology, and the *ballet blanc* supplants the anacreontic interlude. Dancing becomes a transcendental language, charged with spirituality and mystery: a celestial calligraphy, it admits nothing profane.'

André Levinson in *Marie Taglioni*, 1930

Hand coloured lithograph after Alfred Edward Chalon RA
Given by Dame Marie Rambert from the Marie Rambert-Ashley Dukes
Collection E 5049–1968 CT5356

Marie Taglioni in *La Sylphide*

'Taglioni did positively appear on the 26th June [1845 at Her Majesty's Theatre], in the very ballet in which she had often won many hearts, viz., *La Sylphide*, and was hailed with all the enthusiasm of old days. No one could be found to say that her former exquisite grace, her floating lightness of step, her bounding strength, had been in the least impaired by time; and whatever may have been the truth, Taglioni was received by general acclamation as the *Déesse de la Danse*.'

Benjamin Lumley in *Reminiscences of the Opera*, 1864

Hand coloured lithograph after Alfred Edward Chalon RA
Given by Dame Marie Rambert from the Marie Rambert-Ashley Dukes
Collection
E 5050–1968 CT5124

COSTUME ESPAGNOL.

Porté par Mlle Fanny Essler dans le Diable boiteux.

Fanny Elssler (1810–84) in the *Cachucha*

The Austrian ballerina's most famous dance was the Spanish *Cachucha* from Jean Coralli's ballet *Le Diable Boîteux* which she performed in an authentic Spanish costume. She became identified with this dance after her first performance in Paris in 1836 and continued to dance it all over Europe and in America to the end of her career.

'At the tips of her rosy fingers quiver ebony castanets. Now she darts forward; the castanets begin their sonorous chatter. With her hands she seems to shake down great clusters of rhythm. How she twists! How she bends! What fire! What voluptuousness! What precision! Her swooping arms toss about her drooping head, her body curves backwards, her white shoulders almost graze the ground. What a charming posture! Would you not say that in that hand which seems to skim the dazzling barrier of the footlights she gathers up all the desires and all the enthusiasm of the spectators.'

Théophile Gautier quoted by André Levinson in *Marie Taglioni*, 1930

Hand coloured lithograph after Achille Devéria
CT 5359

Fanny Cerrito (1817–1909) dancing *La Lituana*, 1840

One of the favourite Romantic ballerinas. Her London debut in 1840 was described by R.H. Barham in one of the *Ingoldsby Legends*:

> Ma'am'selle Cherrytoes
> Sports her merry toes
> Dancing away to the fiddle and flutes
> In what the folks call a 'Lithuanian' in boots

James D'Egville (c.1770–?) as Chiron and André Jean-Jacques Deshayes
(c.1780–1846) as Achilles in *Achille et Déidamie*

D'Egville, an Englishman, was ballet-master at the King's Theatre from 1799 to
1809. He also started an Academy of Dancing to train English soloists because of
the difficulty of bringing French dancers to England during the Napoleonic wars.
Deshayes, a Frenchman, came from a long line of French ballet-masters and dancers. He first appeared in London in 1800 and danced in nearly every season until
1842 when he first produced *Giselle* in England. *Achille et Déidamie* was first performed at the King's Theatre in 1804.

Hand coloured etching and aquatint
Given by Dame Marie Rambert from the Marie Rambert-Ashley Dukes
Collection
E 4973–1968 CT1011

Margot Fonteyn and Rudolf Nureyev (b. 1938) rehearsing *Giselle* at the Royal Opera House, 1962

It was in *Giselle* in 1962 that Fonteyn first danced with Rudolf Nureyev, and so began a legendary partnership. At what should have been the end of her dancing career, she found new impetus in the young Russian's approach, and over the next few years they were to become the most publicised dance partnership in history. Her English restraint and harmony of movement were the perfect foil to his extrovert passion and animal magnetism, and the controlled abandon of his dancing.

Photograph by Houston Rogers

Adeline Genée (1878–1970) as Camargo in *La Camargo* at the
London Coliseum, 1912

A Danish dancer who came to London in 1897, Genée was the leading dancer at the
Empire Theatre for 10 years. In 1920 she helped found the Royal Academy of
Dancing and became its first president. Created DBE in 1950, she resigned her
Presidency in 1954 and was succeeded by Margot Fonteyn.

'Adeline Genée was the first to fight the strong remains of Victorian prejudice,
not only by the purity of her art, but by her high spiritual integrity. She won not
only admiration for herself and for the art she represented, but genuine respect.'

Tamara Karsavina in *Theatre Street*, 1930

Genée's Camargo costume is in the Museum's collection.

Photograph GK 5599

Margot Fonteyn (b. 1919) in *Aida* with the Vic-Wells Opera at Sadler's Wells
Theatre, 1935

Fonteyn joined the Vic-Wells (now Royal) Ballet in 1934, when the dancers appeared in the opera ballets at Sadler's Wells as well as in the ballet evenings. She attracted attention as the Creole Girl in Frederick Ashton's ballet to Constant Lambert's *Rio Grande*. Until her retirement she remained the greatest English-trained *prima ballerina*, dancing all the major classics and creating leads in most of Ashton's ballets. In her he found the ideal interpreter of his lyrical, understated style, and the roles he made on her at once enshrined her particular qualities and a new, distinctively English school of dancing. Her partnership with Robert Helpmann during the 1930s and 1940s was largely responsible for making ballet a popular art form in England.

Photograph by J.W. Debenham
GJ1972

Marie Rambert (1888–1982) with Frederick Ashton (b. 1904)
in Ashton's ballet *A Tragedy of Fashion*, 1926

A Tragedy of Fashion, presented in the revue *Riverside Nights*, marked an extraordinary double – it was the first work given by the dancers who were to form the nucleus of the Ballet Club (later Ballet Rambert) and the first ballet by Frederick Ashton, who was to become England's greatest choreographer. The driving force behind both the company and Ashton's early work was Polish-born Marie Rambert. Over the next three decades she was to develop a near-miraculous gift for seeking out and developing choreographic talent within her company – in the 1930s she nursed the early works of Antony Tudor, Andrée Howard and Walter Gore, in the 1940s Frank Staff, in the 1950s Norman Morrice, and in the 1960s Christopher Bruce.

Photograph by Yevonde

Ninette de Valois (b. 1898)

Irish-born dancer and choreographer Ninette de Valois made her debut as a dancer in pantomime in 1914, and joined Diaghilev's Ballets Russes in 1923. At a time when ballet was considered the prerogative of the Russians, she believed in the possibility of a British Ballet Company, and to achieve this end she founded a school. In 1926 she offered her students to Lilian Baylis to appear in operas and plays at the Old Vic: in 1931 they established the Vic-Wells (later Sadler's Wells) Ballet. De Valois aimed at developing a company based on the classics, but which would encourage modern ballet and foster native talents in choreography, music and design. By 1956 her original six dancers had grown into two full companies and a school, and the grant of a Royal Charter designated them The Royal Ballet.

Photograph by Gordon Anthony
GF2064

Yvonne Hall and Augustus van Heerden in George Balanchine's ballet *The Four Temperaments*, with Dance Theatre of Harlem, 1984

Photograph by Graham Brandon

Arthur Mitchell faced immense prejudice when he set out to establish a negro classical dance company. He also began by founding a school, which opened in 1968; in 1971 the Dance Theatre of Harlem gave its first public performance, and it has now grown into one of the world's leading companies, drawing on the best of the American ballet repertory and creating new works with their roots in negro traditions and culture.

Costume design for the Entry of Music in the *Ballet des Fées de la Forest de Saint Germain* by Daniel Rabel, 1625

The Court Ballets of the time of Louis XIII were mounted with all the splendour that the French Court could muster. They were immensely popular – a mixture of music, singing, recitation, dance, pantomime and ceremonial processions, augmented by spectacular technical effects and sumptuous scenery and costumes. They were also hugely expensive, the *Ballet des Fées de la Forest de Saint Germain* being one of the most expensive of all. It was a burlesque, organised around the idea of games, and the costumes were wildly inventive, covered with symbols of the characters or allegorical figures that they represented. This design was for the leader of the country musicians who followed the Fairy of Music at the beginning of the ballet.

Pencil, pen and ink and watercolour
CT15176

Gaetano Vestris (1729–1808) as Jason with Mme Simonet as Medea and Giovanna Baccelli as Creusa in the ballet *Medée et Jason*, 1781

The original choreography for this ballet was by Jean Georges Noverre (1727–1810). By the middle of the 18th century the art of ballet had declined into a succession of meaningless dances. It was Noverre who first defined the expressive and dramatic possibilities of dance in his *Lettres sur la Danse* in 1760. He 'advocated unity of design and a logical progression from introduction to climax in which the whole was not sacrificed to the part and all that was unnecessary to the theme was eliminated.' His reforming theories, however, were not truly realised until Fokine began to work with Diaghilev's Ballets Russes.

Vestris, nicknamed 'le dieu de la danse' created the part of Jason in 1763 and revised it for his appearances at the King's Theatre in 1781. Tradition has it that his popularity was so great that a sitting of Parliament had to be suspended to allow Members to attend one of his performances.

Etching and aquatint
E 2836–1962 Z1661

Front-cloth used by Diaghilev for the ballet *Le Train Bleu*, 1924

Copied from a gouache by Pablo Picasso by the scene painter Prince Shervashidze, this image became one of the symbols of the Ballets Russes. Picasso was so pleased with the result that he wrote a dedication to Diaghilev on the cloth. The original gouache is in the Picasso Museum in Paris.

Friends of the Museum of Performing Arts Collection, acquired with funds given by Lord Grade

CT5943

Left Poster for Diaghilev's first Ballets Russes season in Paris, 1909

The illustration for the poster is a reproduction of a drawing by Valentin Serov (1865–1911) of Anna Pavlova (1881–1931) in Fokine's *Les Sylphides*.

Colour lithograph
Given by Richard Buckle CBE, to whom it was given by Lucienne Astruc in memory of her father Gabriel

Tamara Karsavina as Zobeida in
Rimsky-Korsakov's *Schéhérazade*, 1911

Schéhérazade, with choreography by Michel Fokine, was first performed in 1910 with Ida Rubinstein as Zobeida. Karsavina may have lacked Rubinstein's exoticism, but her alluring beauty made her the natural successor to the role.

Postcard photograph

One of the greatest dancers of all time, Karsavina made her debut at the Maryinsky Theatre in 1902. She was the leading dancer in the early years of the Diaghilev Ballets Russes, and often returned to dance for him in later years. Her beauty and intelligence made her the ideal interpreter of Michel Fokine's ballets, and he created many important roles for her, including the title role in *The Firebird*, first performed in Paris in 1910.

'One cannot visualise Diaghileff's ballets at that time without Karsavina. She was indeed the "star". She deserved her great success. Gradually, not only by dancing but by hard work she developed into a ballerina of the first magnitude, technically perfect and a true dramatic artiste. Her own charming personality, fairy-like, poetic, and idealogical, never failed to reach across the footlights.' Prince Peter Lieven in *The Birth of Ballets-Russes*, 1936

Photograph by Bert
Valentine Gross Archive
given by Jean Hugo
HA3388

Tamara Karsavina (1885–1978) in the title role of Stravinsky's *The Firebird*

Serge Diaghilev (1872–1929)

The legendary Russian impresario who revolutionised the art of ballet in the West.

'You were impressed by his manner – quiet and lazy and in some way condescending – the manner of a very important and rather bored *grand seigneur*. He did not abandon this manner of nonchalant importance and apparent indifference even when speaking to the great people of this world or when he was in desperate need of something he was trying to attain. At the same time, and especially in his latter years, he was exquisitely polite, ever a man of breeding and culture; but he was a master in making felt through his politeness the weight of his own importance and his utter self-confidence.'

Prince Peter Lieven
in *The Birth of Ballets-Russes*, 1936

'There is no toxin of sentimentality in Diaghileff. Not only does he not regret yesterday, but all his mental attitude is tending towards to-morrow. He does not treasure relics, he does not turn back to look at the past. In this may lie the explanation of his untiring creative power.'

Tamara Karsavina in *Theatre Street*, 1930

Photograph by Sasha
Given by Nadia Nerina
GE6052

Vaslav Nijinsky as the Faun in *L'Après-midi d'un faune*

The head is the original and only cast of the only sculptured portrait of Nijinsky done from life. No-one knew of its existence until 1954, just before the opening of the great Diaghilev Exhibition in London. Lydia Sokolova saw, among the miscellaneous junk outside an antique shop, a plaster head which she immediately recognised as being Nijinsky as the Faun. She paid 10/- (50p) for it and gave it to Richard Buckle for the Exhibition. It was John Gielgud who remembered seeing a marble version of the head in the possession of Una, Lady Troubridge, and she confirmed that she was the sculptress. Diaghilev hated Nijinsky to sit for artists, but Lady Troubridge arranged with Cecchetti for Nijinsky to sit for her during class, and during performance she worked in the wings. The first Diaghilev knew about it was when the marble, done from the plaster, was exhibited.

Plaster head by Una, Lady Troubridge
Given by Richard Buckle, CBE
Photograph by Graham Brandon

Sketch by Vaslav Nijinsky, 1911

Diaghilev brought the Ballets Russes to London for the Coronation season of 1911, and was immediately lionised by London's high bohemian society, among them Mrs Enthoven. It was during one of her visits to see Diaghilev at the Savoy Hotel that Nijinsky made for her a little sketch of a dancer in the *Polovtsian Dances* from *Prince Igor*. Early drawings by Nijinsky are extremely rare, although drawings made after his mental decline are widely known.

Pencil
GK2630

SAVOY HOTEL,
LONDON.

Prince Igor.
Drawn by Nijinsky while talking to
Diaghileff and me at the Savoy Hotel.

Gabrielle Enthoven.
July 5ᵗʰ 1911

Vaslav Nijinsky, 1939

'A *barre* had been installed in the room and Lifar exercised at it in front of Vaslav, who responded by nodding, tapping his foot and counting. When Lifar danced part of *L'Après-midi d'un faune*, Vaslav pushed him aside and corrected him. Other dances he applauded. But when Lifar tried a bit of *Le Spectre de la rose*, as if in reaction to the *entrechats*, Nijinsky without *préparation* or *plié*, rose from the floor in a high jump, laughing. A photographer was present and recorded this unexpected though hoped-for feat.'

Richard Buckle in *Nijinsky*, 1975

Photograph from a magazine

Adolph Bolm (1884–1951) as the Polovtsian Chief in *The Polovtsian Dances* from Borodin's opera *Prince Igor*, 1909

The sensation of the first night of the Ballets Russes in Paris in 1909 was the *Polovtsian Dances*. The wild, uninhibited savagery of Fokine's choreography, the pounding rhythms of the music and the chanting chorus whipped the audience into a virtual frenzy. No one in Paris could have conceived of men dancing with such virile power and attack. To them the male dancer was a figure of ridicule, his roles usually taken by a shapely girl *en travesti*. Almost overnight their attitude changed. Much of the credit for that change of mind must go to Adolph Bolm whose performance as the Warrior Chief was at the centre of Fokine's highly-choreographed disorder. Dancing as if possessed, his performance symbolised the 'spontaneity, passion and proud freedom of the nomadic tribes' – '. . . beautiful and bloody; he is the Germ of Destruction, the Spirit of Unrest . . . It is terrible but it is magnificent; it is barbarous, it is the alpha and omega of human existence; for it is war.'

Arthur Applin in *The Stories of the Russian Ballet*, 1911

Bronze by Frödman-Cluzel
Cyril Beaumont Bequest
Photograph by Graham Brandon

Portrait of Leonide Massine (1895–1979) by Pablo Picasso (1881–1973)

This drawing was made in Rome in 1917 when Picasso was designing *Parade*.

Pencil
S.308–1980 HB20

Costume design by Pablo Picasso for the Chinese Conjuror in *Parade*

The ballet, with choreography by Massine (who also danced the part of the Chinese
Conjuror), was first performed in Paris in 1917. It was Picasso's first work for the
stage and the first time that the Cubist style was used for the theatre.
The original costume is in the collections of the Museum.

Pen and ink
HD3683

With best wishes
to M? King.
from Alicia Markova
Diaghileff Russian Ballet
1928.

Igor Stravinsky (1882–1971) playing *Le Sacre du Printemps*
Caricature by Jean Cocteau

Pen and ink
S.307–1980 HA3500

Alicia Markova (b.1910) as the Nightingale in Stravinsky's *Le Chant du Rossignol*, 1927

The ballet was adapted by Stravinsky from his opera *Le Rossignol* and was first produced in 1920 with choreography by Leonide Massine and designs by Henri Matisse. In 1925, as everyone had forgotten the choreography, George Balanchine choreographed a new version, his first ballet for Diaghilev. Markova had joined the Diaghilev Ballets Russes in 1925 and first danced the Nightingale in 1927. She was so small that the original costume was totally unsuitable, and a new one had to be made for her by Vera Soudeikina (who was later to marry Stravinsky) under the supervision of Matisse. Matisse wanted a fitted bonnet decorated with osprey feathers, which Diaghilev declared would be far too expensive. In the end Matisse and Stravinsky had to share the cost between them.

Photograph
Given by William Beaumont Morris
HA3482

Vaslav Nijinsky (1890–1950) as the Golden Slave in Rimsky-Korsakov's *Schéhérazade*, 1910

Photograph by Bert
CT10108

Serge Lifar (1905–1986) as Apollo in Stravinsky's *Apollon musagète*

Photograph
HA3375

Olga Spessivtseva (b.1895) as Princess Aurora in
The Sleeping Princess with Léon Bakst (1866–1924)

Photograph
GK2628

'When I came into the studio with Diaghilev, Spessivtseva was working at the barre ... She began to rehearse Aurora's variation. The others, who were working all over the room, stopped one by one and stood motionless, watching her dance. Smiling, she moved with an extraordinary serenity and ease, and the virtuoso steps she was executing seemed simple and natural. She never had to reach for balance; she seemed sustained by an invisible thread. At the end of the variation, there was a long, admiring silence, and then the room exploded into applause ...'

Boris Kochno
in *Diaghilev and the Ballets Russes*, 1970

Bakst was one of the most original designers in the history of theatre. His designs for *Schéhérazade* for the Ballets Russes in 1910 created a sensation. The daring contrasts of bold colours, reds, greens, blues, yellows which he used for the set and the costumes had never been seen on a stage before. *The Sleeping Princess* was his last glorious production for Diaghilev.

Costume design by Léon Bakst for Anna Pavlova in *Ballet Hindou*, 1913

Pencil and watercolour
Cyril Beaumont Bequest
CT9503

Anna Pavlova (1881–1931) as the
Swan in *Le Cygne*, 1928

In Pavlova's interpretation, Fokine's
deceptively simple solo became a
moving expression of the swan's
fight against death, combining grace
and despair yet great strength as life
ebbed away. The solo became
completely identified with Pavlova,
and in her own mind swans became a
special symbol to her – she kept
several almost as pets at her London
home. As she lay dying, almost her
final words were to her maid, asking
that her Swan tutu be got ready.
Two days after she died, at a performance in London, the audience
stood in silence before a darkened
stage, lit only by a single spotlight,
while the orchestra played *Le Cygne*
– a unique tribute to a unique artist.

Photograph by Nicholas Yarovoff
HA200

Alicia Markova in *Giselle*, Act II,
c.1937

Markova first danced Giselle with
the Vic-Wells (now Royal) Ballet
in 1934, the first English dancer
ever to undertake the role. After
Diaghilev's death, Markova did a
great deal to help establish ballet in
England, appearing with the
Camargo Society and the Ballet Club
(now Ballet Rambert) and becoming
first ballerina of the Vic-Wells Ballet.
From the mid-1930s, in a famous
partnership with Anton Dolin, she
won a new public for ballet in
England, first with the Markova-
Dolin Ballet, which they founded in
1935, then with Festival Ballet,
which they founded in 1951.

Photograph by Gilbert Adams

Emma Livry (1842–63) in *La Sylphide*

A pupil of Marie Taglioni, she made her debut in *La Sylphide* in Paris in 1858.
Taglioni saw Livry as her natural successor but in 1862, during a rehearsal, Livry's
dress caught fire from brushing against a candle and she was severely burnt. She
died in agony eight months later.

Hard paste porcelain, French, 1861
Cyril W. Beaumont Bequest

and Fanny Elssler in the *Cachucha*

Bronze by Barre
Given by Richard Buckle CBE

Photograph by Graham Brandon

Loie Fuller (1862–1928)

American dancer, revolutionary in her integration of costume and light in her performances. Wearing and manipulating masses of diaphanous silk, dancing on a darkened stage without decor, or on a glass floor lit from below, she expertly handled her costumes so that they rippled delicately, or became huge sculptural shapes. Shape and form changed with the lights as they flowed across the silk. She was acclaimed in Paris by artists of every school, but her swirling, seemingly natural art was especially attuned to the Art Nouveau movement; she inspired many craftsmen, and lives on in sculptures, lamps and artefacts of all kinds.

Marble
Photograph by Graham Brandon

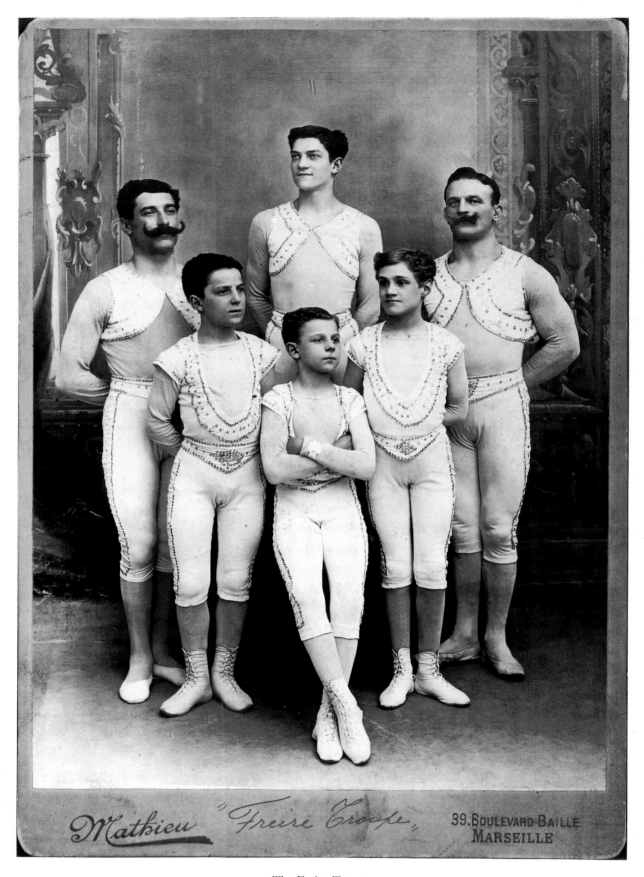

The Freire Troupe

STAR TURNS

'This, then, is the Great Actor's secret, that he can feel an emotion so intensely, express it so vividly, and share it with his audience so completely, that he turns a crowd of strangers, for the moment, into a sentient being.'

W.A. Darlington

'Buy a bill of the play'

Hand coloured etching
CT4940

Playbill for the Theatre Royal,
Covent Garden, 1 June 1814

Harry R. Beard Collection
S71

Kate Vaughan (c.1852–1903) as
Lady Teazle in *The School for Scandal*
by Richard Brinsley Sheridan (1751–1816),
at the Opéra Comique, London, 1887

Kate Vaughan made her reputation as a skirt dancer and as a burlesque actress.
From 1876 to 1883 she was a member of the famous Gaiety Quartet, with Nellie
Farren, Edward Terry and Royce, but she then abandoned dancing to act and
manage her own Company, specialising in the classic English comedies.

'Miss Kate Vaughan's reading of Lady Teazle is one of the most original, and in
many points most satisfactory, of the many modern readings of the part. No one
should go away with the impression that it is a pretty Lady Teazle because her
representative dances and dresses well. It is no new success of the costumier, or the
toes. It is an understandable woman, and a very human one, after all.'

Contemporary review

Photograph by W. & D. Downey
Guy Little Collection
CT10156

Right
Mrs H. Johnson in *Timour the Tartar*

Hand coloured etching
Harry R. Beard Collection
HRB F24–11 CT4038

Playbill for Theatre Royal, Covent Garden,
15 May 1811

Harry R. Beard Collection
SH117

Timour the Tartar by Monk Lewis at the
Theatre Royal, Covent Garden, 1811

A very popular piece 'in which Astley's fine
horses were exhibited on the stage with surprising effect'. As somebody said at the time: 'It's
no wonder that *Timour the Tartar* should be performed every night to overflowing houses,
when it is considered that horses are so well
calculated to draw!'

'Tuppence coloured' sheet published by
Creed
Hand coloured etching
CT3788

Mʳˢ H-JOHNSTON, in the MELODRAMA of
TIMOUR the TARTAR.
Pubᵈ by Dighton, Spring Gardens, June, 1811.

Rex Harrison (b.1908) as Professor Higgins and Julie Andrews (b.1935) as Eliza
Doolittle in *My Fair Lady*, the musical play by Alan Jay Lerner and Frederick
Loewe based on Shaw's *Pygmalion* at the Theatre Royal, Drury Lane, 1958

'But *My Fair Lady* was never profligate: it may be the only musical play in which
the hero and heroine never kiss or embrace. It had another distinction. The score
was not only infectiously melodious, but it served the play with a kind of selfless
dedication, as if it were more interested in the play than its own success. It por-
trayed character: it accelerated the momentum of the narrative and also gave the
audience enormous pleasure. *My Fair Lady* was brilliantly staged by Moss Hart at
the peak of his ability; and the part of Henry Higgins was brilliantly played by Rex
Harrison with virtuosity and subtleties of inflection that brought wit and humour
into a romantic story.'

Brooks Atkinson in *Broadway*, 1970

Photograph by Cecil Beaton

Mrs Patrick Campbell (*née* Beatrice Stella Tanner, 1865–1940) as Eliza Doolittle
in Shaw's *Pygmalion*, 1914

'The part of Eliza was written for Mrs Campbell. There are passages in it which
could only have been written by a dramatist who delighted in the temperament of
that great actress as well as in her art; and was set on using, not only her unrivalled
grace and elocution, but a strain of Italian peasant in her: she would make, he saw, a
perfect flower-girl as well as a perfect lady, while remaining patently herself. I have
been told ... that when Mr Shaw first read the play aloud, she cried out at one
point, "You wretch! That's *me*." No other actress could have smoothed so perfectly Eliza's manners, or have flung Higgins' slippers in his face with such spirit.'
Desmond MacCarthy in *Shaw: The Plays*, 1973

Photograph published in *The Sketch*, 22 April 1914 GH2696

Kate Terry (1844–1924) – an Andromeda study

Kate was Ellen Terry's older sister and, in the opinion of many, the finer actress of the two. She was on stage from childhood, becoming a great star in the provinces, but she left the stage on her marriage in 1867. Her daughter, also Kate, was the mother of John Gielgud. Although best known as the author of *Alice in Wonderland*, the Rev. C.L. Dodgson was also a brilliant amateur photographer. This photograph was probably inspired by Kate's performance as Andromeda in the burlesque *Perseus and Andromeda; or the Maids and the Monster* by W. Brangl, which she played at the St. James's Theatre in 1861.

Photograph by Lewis Carroll (Rev. C.L. Dodgson)

Mrs Pope, in the Character of Zara.

Engraved by Saillier, from the original Picture, which was painted from life, by De Wilde, from the Mourning Bride, by Congreve, in the Celebrated Edition of Bell's British Theatre, which is now Publishing Periodically.

THE PASSAGE
—— but when I feel
These bonds, I look with loathing on myself.

Printed for J. Bell British Library London Dec.ʳ 6ᵗʰ 1791.

Jane Pope (1742–1818) in the title role of *Zara* by Voltaire (François Marie Arouet), 1791

Jane Pope had played as a child with Garrick, but her adult debut was in 1759, as Corinna in *The Confederacy*. Her success was such that she was soon regarded as the natural successor to Kitty Clive, playing hoydens, chambermaids and pert ladies with a brilliance that made Churchill call her 'lively Pope'. She was the original Mrs Candour in *The School for Scandal* and Tilburina in *The Critic*.

Hand coloured stipple engraving
Harry R. Beard Collection
F74–29 CT4358

Sarah Siddons (1755–1831) as Euphrasia in *The Grecian Daughter* by Arthur
Murphy, 1782

'The person of Mrs Siddons rather courted the regal attire, and her beauty became
more vivid from the decorations of her rank. The commanding height and powerful action of her figure, though always feminine, seemed to tower beyond her sex.
Till this night we had not heard the full extent, nor much of the quality of her
voice. An opportunity occurred even in the first act, to throw out some of its most
striking tones.'

James Boaden in *Memoirs of Mrs Siddons*, 1827

Engraving
GG5775

Sybil Thorndike (1882–1976) as Hecuba in *The Trojan Women* by Euripides
at the Old Vic, 1919

'... Miss Sybil Thorndike as Medea reaches great heights. Her gestures, her facial
play, her raucous tones, her alternations of pathetic softness and shrill exasper-
ation, are all in the true tragic style, and yet in the whirlwind of her passion there is
no lapse from beauty. It is a great achievement.'

The Sketch, 1919

Sybil Thorndike was one of the most loved of English actresses, not just as a brilliant performer, but also as
a compassionate human being. The foundations of her career were laid with Miss Horniman's Gaiety
Theatre in Manchester (where she met and married Lewis Casson) and during the First World War, at the
Old Vic, where her downright, commonsense Christianity endeared her to Lilian Baylis. She played every
conceivable form of theatre – Shakespeare, Greek tragedy, modern drama, drawing-room comedies, poetic
drama and Grand Guignol – bringing to all her roles an invigorating sense of moral purpose. This made her
the perfect interpreter of Shaw's heroines; she was, he said, his ideal Candida, and in 1924 he wrote St Joan
for her, which became the outstanding success of her career.

Photograph by Florence Vandamm
GK4524

Left above
Michael Redgrave (1908–85) as Rakitin in *A Month in the Country* by Ivan Turgenev, translated by
Constance Garnett, at the New Theatre, 1949

'His performance is exemplary. His Rakitin stands, so to speak, at just that distance from himself that the
ironist commonly keeps (so long as he is untouched); and when he moves into passion it is with an
admirably restrained intensity that leaves us feeling as we should about all these people: Ah, the self-
absorbtion of them all.'

T.C. Worsley in the *New Statesman and Nation*, 31 December 1949

Photograph by John Vickers

Right above George Alexander (1858–1918) as Silvio in *The Amber Heart* by Alfred C. Calmour at the
Lyceum Theatre, 1888

George Alexander joined Irving's Lyceum company in 1881. Although it was an excellent training ground,
life at the Lyceum was not easy for young actors, and after five or six hours of Irving's rehearsals, Alexander
would go home almost in tears: 'and I made up my mind that if I ever had a company of my own I would let
them down pretty easy.' In 1891 he took over the St. James's Theatre, which he ran until his death. During
his management his policy was to encourage English playwrights, and among the eighty new plays he
produced were *The Second Mrs Tanqueray*, *His House in Order*, *Lady Windermere's Fan*, and *The Importance of
Being Earnest*. An excellent actor of great charm, with a light touch in comedy (he was the first John
Worthing), a fine romantic presence in costume drama and restrained dignity in modern plays. He was also
an excellent businessman, and made the St. James's one of the most successful theatres in London.

Photograph by Window & Grove
GE6385

Left below Henry Irving as Mephistopheles in *Faust* by W.G. Wills, from Goethe's tragedy,
at the Lyceum Theatre, 1885

'Although the inadequacy of the text was plain to all, although Irving's most ardent admirers admitted that
his demon teetered dangerously on the edge of pantomime, and although the whole affair offended the
genuine and professed students of Goethe, this consummate confection of villainy and piety, of beauty and
fearsome hideousness, of claptrap and culture, was the greatest financial success Irving ever had. ... It
would be idle to pretend that he and Ellen Terry did not delight in this histrionic romp. He probably
enjoyed every one of the seven hundred appearances he made as Mephistopheles.'

Laurence Irving in *Henry Irving*, 1951

Watercolour by Bernard Partridge
CT10136

Right below Donald Wolfit (1902–68) in the title role of *Tamburlaine* by Christopher Marlowe
at the Old Vic, 1951

'There has never been an actor of greater gusto than Wolfit: he has dynamism, energy, bulk and stature, and
he joins these together with a sheer relish for resonant words which splits small theatres as Caruso shattered
wine glasses.'

Kenneth Tynan in *A View of the English Stage*, 1975

Photograph by John Vickers
GJ1815

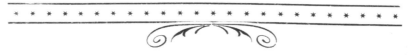

Mr Henry Irving as Mephistopheles

Left above Ralph Richardson as Cherry in *Flowering Cherry* by Robert Bolt,
at the Theatre Royal, Haymarket, 1957

'Sir Ralph excels in studies of suburban shipwreck. As the average man submerging in the sea of life, his round, moon-struck face looms up with a bemused pathos, and his flat, slurred voice drones out above the flotsam of cliché with a ring of poetry.... Sir Ralph presents a wage-slave of an insurance firm, drunk with gin, "scrumpy" and dreams of Country Life, whose world has come to grief on the rocks of reality. Sir Ralph haloes this tedious shammer with a luminous authority, demonstrating the individual talents for comedy, pathos and even – at moments – tragedy ...'

Richard Findlater in the Sunday Despatch, 24 November 1957

Photograph by Angus McBean
Hugh Beaumont Collection

Right above Herbert Beerbohm Tree as Svengali in *Trilby* by Paul Potter,
based on Du Maurier's novel, Theatre Royal, Haymarket, 1895

'It was a masterpiece of eerie, bizarre fantasy, a superb realisation of every evil and grotesque quality with which Du Maurier endowed his picture of fantastic villainy.... no Svengali in my experience has managed to convey anything like the floridity, the mocking, insolent assurance, the swagger, the half-veiled animosity, the odious conceit, that Tree expressed. It was, without doubt, the most outstanding part of his career and, as a piece of character acting, has rarely been bettered by any other actor in whatever creation.'

A.E. Wilson in Edwardian Theatre

Photograph by Alfred Ellis
GH1176

Left below John Gielgud as Raskolnikov in *Crime and Punishment*, a dramatisation by Rodney Ackland
of the novel by Feodor Dostoevsky, New Theatre, 1946

'... John Gielgud, easily our best player at suggesting a man living entirely on his nerves. All actors have their physical limitations, and Mr Gielgud has his share ... In the present play Mr Gielgud makes his limitations work for instead of against him. The result is the best thing after Hamlet he has ever given us.'

The Sunday Times, 30 June 1947

Photograph by Alexander Bender
Hugh Beaumont Collection

Right below Gerald du Maurier (1873–1934) as the Duc de Charmerace in *Arsène Lupin* from the French
by Francis de Croisset and Maurice Leblanc at the Duke of York's Theatre, 1909

'Actually Gerald du Maurier, brilliant actor that he was, had the most disastrous influence on my generation, because we really thought, looking at him, that it was easy; and for the first ten years of our lives in the theatre nobody could hear a word we said. We thought he was being really natural; of course he was a genius of a technician giving that appearance, that's all.'

Laurence Olivier in Great Acting, edited by Hal Burton, 1967

Photograph by Foulsham & Banfield
GG5818

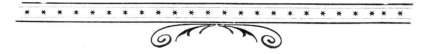

Noël Coward (1899–1973) and Gertrude Lawrence (1898–1952) in *Shadowplay*
from *Tonight at 8.30* by Noël Coward at the Phoenix Theatre, 1936

Although their names are linked in the public mind, Coward and Gertrude
Lawrence only played together on stage twice – in *Private Lives* and the series of
one-act plays that made up *Tonight at 8.30*. They had been friends since childhood,
when they had appeared in the chorus of a production of Hauptmann's *Hannele* at
Liverpool. Coward recalled his first impressions:

'... a vivacious child with ringlets to whom I took an instant fancy. ... her face
was far from pretty, but tremendously alive. ... She confided to me that her name
was Gertrude Lawrence, but that I was to call her Gert because everybody did ...
She then gave me a few mild dirty stories, and I loved her from then onwards.'

Noël Coward in *Present Indicative*, 1940

Photograph by Leadley-Dallison
Given by Mrs Hugh Baker

Noël Coward by Gladys Calthrop, 1930s
Pencil and watercolour
Given by the executors of the Gladys Calthrop Estate

Donald Sinden as Sir Harcourt Courtly in *London Assurance* by Dion Boucicault
at the Aldwych Theatre, 1970

'Donald Sinden's Sir Harcourt ... resembles Oscar Wilde simultaneously playing George IV and the Apollo Belvedere. Mr Sinden's presence and wit, his insolent yet apprehensive stares, and his immense style are the centre of the play.'

Harold Hobson in *The Sunday Times*, 28 June 1970

Photograph by Zoë Dominic

W.S. Penley (1852–1912) as Lord Fancourt Babberley in *Charley's Aunt* by
Brandon Thomas at the Royalty Theatre, 1892

'There was the usual excitement before the curtain rose and it was not long before ripples of laughter spread through the auditorium. Penley as Lord Fancourt Babberley ... was warmly received on his first entrance, and soon the laughter grew louder. But when Charley's real aunt failed to appear and "Babs" took her place, it was as though lightning had struck the theatre. Penley's appearance in the now familiar black satin dress, complete with bonnet, fichu and mittens, stopped the show. For it was 1892, you must remember, and in the stalls could be seen plenty of real chaperones, each and every one the spit and image of "Charley's Aunt". The fireman laughed so much he fell against the bell and rang the curtain down in the middle of the act. The Duke of Cambridge was so overcome that his stall collapsed beneath him and he remained sitting on the floor, speechless with mirth.'

Souvenir of *Charley's Aunt*, 1952

Within a month the Royalty was too small to hold the play, and it transferred to the larger old Globe Theatre. Twelve thousand pounds in advance bookings were taken in the first week and huge traffic jams built up every night. The play ran for 1,466 continuous performances, a record for the time. It was produced all over the world – at one time it was being played in forty-eight theatres on the same night – and translated into Afrikaans, Japanese, Welsh, Zulu and Esperanto.

Photograph by T.C. Turner
GG3838

GRIMALDI & the NONDESCRIPT in the Red Dwarf

the Clown kills the Pantaloon, and afterwards Dresses him in the Skin of a Lion, the Head of an Ass, Eagles Wings, Cats feet & a Fishes tail

Joseph Grimaldi (1779–1837) in *The Red Dwarf* at the Theatre Royal, Drury Lane.

'As a *Clown*, Grimaldi is perfectly unrivalled. Other performers of the part may be droll in their generation; but, which of them can for a moment compete with the Covent-Garden hero in acute observation upon the foibles and absurdities of society, and his happy talent of holding them up to ridicule? He is the finest practical satirist that ever existed. He does not, like many clowns, content himself with raising a horse-laugh by contortions and grimaces, but tickles the fancy and excites the risibility of an audience by devices as varied as they are ingenious.'

From *The Biography of the British Stage*, 1824

Hand coloured etching
Harry R. Beard Collection
HRB67–32 CT5362

Harry Payne (1831–1895)

Harry Payne was a pantomime clown, appearing in the Harlequinades that were a feature of 19th-century pantomime, and which could still occasionally be seen in the present century.

Colour lithograph by Jules Cheret, signed and dedicated 1868 (?3)
Harry R. Beard Collection F75–31
CT6103

Coco (1900—74)

'It was during the Manchester season (1929) that Coco had his first contract with
Bertram Mills. Father had seen him in the Busch Circus in Berlin and given him a
four-week contract as a run-in clown. Little did either of them think that the
contract would be renewed over and over again so that it eventually covered all the
ensuing summer and winter seasons over a period of thirty-seven years ... It may
be worth noting that he is always referred to as Coco the Clown, but in circus
terminology this is incorrect. A clown is the white-faced man in the magnificent
spangled costume, but the man who, like Coco, is always at the receiving end when
water and custard pies are flying is an Auguste.'

Cyril Mills in *Bertram Mills Circus: its story*, 1967

Photograph
GG788

Dany Renz at Bertram
Mills Circus, Olympia,
1955

The Renz circus dynasty
goes back to 1843 and was
primarily concerned with
horses and riding. Renz
married Sabine Rancy
thus uniting two famous
circus families.

Photograph by Baron
Nicholas de Rakoczy

Con Colleano

'The greatest wire-walker the world has ever
seen was Con Colleano. In fact, he was more
than a wire-walker; he picked up the threads
of the old tradition and, adapting them to the
pattern of today, showed us what the term
rope-dancer really meant . . . But Colleano was a
wire-dancer. His footwork was superb. His
greatest feat was a forward somersault, which
is much more difficult than a backward one.
In turning forward through the air you cannot see where to put your feet as you land,
while in throwing a back somersault the eyes
can see both the feet and the wire as the head
comes up.'

Antony Hippisley Coxe
in *A Seat at the Circus*, 1951, revised 1980

Photograph
Antony Hippisley Coxe Circus Collection

Schumann horse at Bertram Mills Circus, Olympia,
1958

'The greatest horse trainers in the world, however, are
still the Schumanns. There is a saying on the Continent
that when a Schumann cracks his whip even a wooden
horse will dance.'

Antony Hippisley Coxe
in *A Seat at the Circus*, 1951, revised 1980

Photograph by Baron Nicholas de Rakoczy

Playbill for Astley's Theatre

Philip Astley (1742–1814) invented the circus in 1768.
He had been a sergeant-major and breaker-in in
General Elliott's Light Horse. He was the first to realise that by galloping in a circle 42 feet in diameter he
could keep his balance standing on a horse's back by
using centrifugal force. As equestrian acts were the
basis on which circus was formed, it takes place in a
ring which is always the same size. If you want a bigger
circus you have to have more rings – hence the famous
Three Ring Circus.

CT4348

Programme for Collins's Music Hall
Harry R. Beard Collection

Music cover for 'Champagne Charlie' with George Leybourne (1842–84)

'Champagne Charlie' established Leybourne as one of the great music-hall stars. The image he set before his working-class audience was a caricature of the West End 'swell' of mid-Victorian London with his monocle and fashionable 'Dundreary' whiskers, gaily coloured waistcoat and trousers, and glistening boots. By 1865 he was a 'top liner' at the Canterbury Hall, Lambeth, at the then enormous salary of £30 a week, but 'Champagne Charlie' consolidated his success and his salary rocketed to £120.

Colour lithograph
Harry R. Beard Collection
CT6920

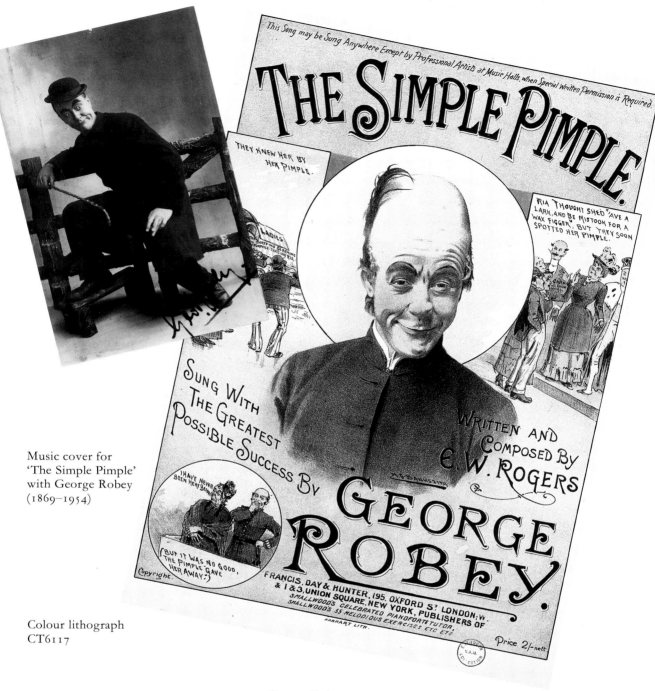

Music cover for
'The Simple Pimple'
with George Robey
(1869–1954)

Colour lithograph
CT6117

George Robey

'But George Robey: one cannot leave out Robey, that black-clad delicious impertinence. Set in the beauty and opulence of the Revue he shines like a black pearl in a coloured tie. He has the grand manner of oddity and we respect his eyebrows, also, he can command an audience with a broken umbrella, half a walking stick or an absurd hat. He adopts the innuendo, he rolls his eyes and he squints. He adopts an almost paternal way with the audience.'

Dion Clayton Calthrop in *Music Hall Nights*, 1925

Signed photograph
GH1165

Vesta Tilley

Signed photograph by
Brown, Barnes & Bell
Guy Little Collection
GH3836

Music cover for 'Burlington Bertie' sung by Vesta Tilley (1864–1952)

'We must remember "Burlington Bertie" because he is the clue to Vesta Tilley's opinion of men. "He'll fight and he'll die like an Englishman," she sang in the midst of her mockery of his follies, which is a plain hint that Vesta Tilley's understanding sympathy for her "victims" has never been very far beneath the surface. That is precisely why we have always been hypnotised by them . . . By pretending to be young men for so long, she had come to understand them as well as they did themselves. Now she went further, and understood them better than they did themselves. That is why we saw them, not as we could see them in real life but as they were when viewed through a clever woman's eyes.'

M. Willson Disher in *Winkles and Champagne*, 1938

Colour lithograph
Harry R. Beard Collection

Marie Lloyd (1870–1922)

'No nonsense about our Marie I tell you
straight. If you don't like it, lump it, and if
not buzz off. She makes no pretence at
character study but is just herself, her own
plump, rollicking self. No one could be
more British. She is the height of vulgarity
with a great heart. Her naughtiness is that
of a child who wishes to shock. It is perfectly harmless, she is merely calling Mrs
Grundy a silly old frump. In Paris she
would be suggestive, evil, here she is open,
perhaps a trifle too frank. Women who
have families and go to Church roar with
laughter and turn pink and hide their con-
vulsed faces with their hands. The chorus
of *Tommy Make Room For Your Uncle* goes
booming through the house. She need not
sing *Oh, Mr Porter, Whatever Shall I Do*, the
house sings it for her. There is nothing like
her, she's London if you like, and she's
beanos down to Epping Forest, horse
char-à-banc, cornet and all, and she's
baked potatoes and barrel organs, and fish
and chips.'

Dion Clayton Calthrop
in *Music Hall Nights*, 1925

Photograph by Hana
Guy Little Collection
CT10157

"Lauder" The real article :.

Harry Lauder (1870–1950)

'His world-wide popularity is not due simply to his efforts, but to the
spark of Burns' fire he inherited at birth . . . Nature seems to have inten-
ded him for caricature, for his face is magnified, and his body, with short
thick legs and tiny squat feet, diminished. Nature was subtle when she
framed him, but he is subtle too . . . For every song he seems to have a
distinct complexion. Compare the blooming cheeks of the exuberant
dandy in kilts, hugging himself with joy at the thought of his lassie, with
the sagging skin and shadowed eyes of the old married man, jubilantly
setting out for a holiday because his wife is in hospital and himself "off
the chain".'

M. Willson Disher in *Winkles and Champagne*, 1938

Photograph
GH2694

127

Dan Leno in the title role of the pantomime *Mother Goose* at the Theatre Royal,
Drury Lane, 1902

'All the evening we have been conscious of the magic name Dan Leno. Great Little
Dan, how we loved him, how we knew every intonation of his voice. If we were
faithful to him, which we were, he was faithful to us. He was the Emperor of Red
Nosed Comedians and gave us that laughter which is akin to tears . . . The simplicity of his humour reads bald in cold print. The "spoken", printed at the end of his
songs conveys nothing when he conveyed so much, but when his genius illumi-
nated the sentences we rocked with laughter. The house in fact lost all control of
itself. Dan had a smile from ear to ear, and bright sparkling eyes and wonderfully
expressive hands and feet.'

Dion Clayton Calthrop in *Music Hall Nights*, 1925

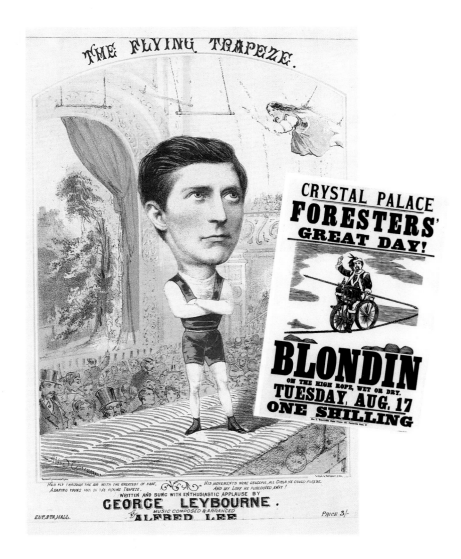

Music cover for 'The Flying Trapeze' with George Leybourne

Leybourne is here seen not as his usual man-about-town self but in the same kind of singlet as worn by Léotard who invented the flying trapeze act in the 1850s.

Colour lithograph
CT6919

Poster advertising Blondin at the Crystal Palace, 1869

Chevalier Blondin (Jean François Gravelet, 1824–97) made his name by crossing the Niagara Falls on a tightrope for the first time on 30 June 1859. He made several crossings, sometimes blindfolded, sometimes pushing a wheelbarrow. Once, he stopped half-way across and fried himself an omelette. Blondin's wheelbarrow is in the collections of the Museum.

HB1277

LE GÉNÉRAL TOM POUCE
14 Ans 67 Cent.

Tom Thumb (Charles S. Stratton, 1832–83) as Napoleon

34 years old and 67 centimetres high. One of Tom Thumb's waistcoats is in the collections of the Museum.

Hand coloured lithograph
GH3319

Gen Tom Thumb

Tom Thumb's visiting card (actual size)

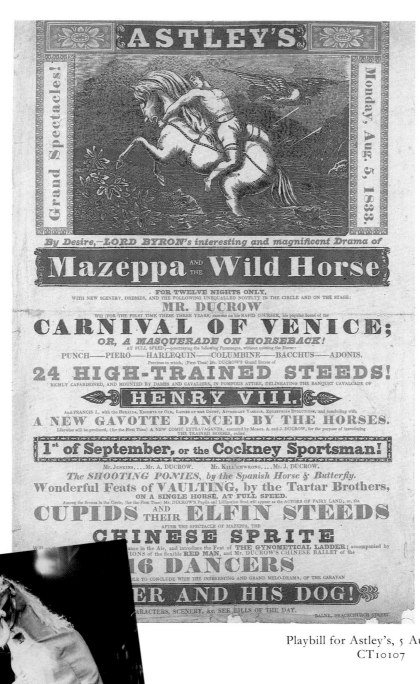

Playbill for Astley's, 5 August 1833
CT10107

Arthur Askey (1900–83) as Widow
Twankey in the pantomime *Aladdin and his
Wonderful Lamp* at the London Palladium,
1964

Photograph by Cyrus Andrews

Music cover for *The Music Man* with Howard Paul, c.1860

Colour lithograph

Mick Jagger (b.1943)

Mick Jagger, lead singer with The Rolling Stones, photographed during their 1972 European tour. The white panne velvet jump-suit was designed by Ossie Clark for the tour and was donated to the museum by Mick Jagger.

Photograph by Pennie Smith

The Beverley Sisters (Babs, Joy and Teddy), 1950s

Fred Astaire (b.1899) and Adele Astaire (1898–1981) in *Stop Flirting* at the
Shaftesbury Theatre, 1923

GG4579

The Beatles – John Lennon (1940–80), Paul McCartney (b.1942) George Harrison (b.1943), Pete Best (b.1943) – photographed in the Cavern, Liverpool, about 1961. The drummer, Pete Best, was replaced by Ringo Starr (b.1940) in August 1972.

David Bowie (b.1947) photographed during his 1973 British tour at the Rollerena Roller Skating Rink, Leeds

Photograph by Kevin Cummins

Cliff Richard (b.1940) and the Shadows (Bruce Welch, Tony Meehan, Jet Harris and Hank B. Marvin)
photographed during their first British tour in 1959

Photograph by John Vane

Elvis Presley (1935–77)

Cibachrome print by Miki Slingsby after a painting 'Elvis Presley: The King – Fairground Sounds' by
David Oxtoby, 1976. The original painting was destroyed, along with 22 others, by thieves in 1979.

Given by David Oxtoby and Vision International

Marie Tempest (1864–1942) in the title role of the comic opera *Dorothy*
by C. Stephenson and A. Cellier at the Gaiety Theatre, 1886

'She touched me, thrilled me, and enchanted me ... I have seen her on occasion
snappy and bad-tempered, particularly with actors whose lack of talent or casual-
ness in the theatre exasperated her. She has a personal imperiousness that demands
good behaviour in others, but if you give in to her too much she'll bully the life out
of you. She is lovable as a person and unique as an artist, and her charm is ageless.'
Noël Coward in *Present Indicative*, 1940

Photograph by Walery
Guy Little Collection
GH3813

Sarah Bernhardt in the title role of *Fedora* by Victorien Sardou

'[She played] with such tigerish passion and feline seduction which, whether it be good or bad art, nobody has been able to match since.'

Maurice Baring in *Sarah Bernhardt*, 1933

Photograph by Nadar

Marie Lloyd (1870–1922)

'I bet if I sang the Songs of Solomon they'd accuse me of making them sound bad!'
Marie Lloyd

Miniature photographs by Alfred Ellis & Walery

Gertie Millar (1880–1952) as Cora Bellamy in the musical play *The Toreador* by
J.T. Tanner and Harry Nicholls, music by Ivan Caryll and Lionel Monckton, at
the Gaiety Theatre, 1901

'... I had adored her; and in my memory she is clearly the most graceful and
charming artiste I have ever seen. Now that I know her well I can never look at her
gay unchanged face without a little stab of the heart, to think that never again will
she float down the stage, chuckling lightly and expressing with her hands a joy of
living which was her own special charm.'
Noël Coward in *Present Indicative*, 1940

Photograph by Alfred Ellis and Walery
GG3842

Gladys Cooper (1888–1971)

Gladys Cooper made her stage debut in 1905, and by 1907 was employed by George Edwardes as one of the famous Gaiety Girls. She divided her time between the theatre and the photographic studios of Foulsham and Banfield, who had her under contract to sit for them once a month. Over five hundred different postcards of her were issued and she became one of the most fashionable faces of the Edwardian era. 'I had almost a monopoly there for a while. Mine was a new face, and they'd put me into ordinary profile shots as special series – I once did a whole series of cards as Juliet though I'd never actually played the part. In the end it became a handicap, being better known on postcards than on the stage, but at the time it was all very helpful, and I was certainly in no position to turn down regular work.'

Quoted by Sheridan Morley in *Gladys Cooper*, 1979

Photograph postcard
GE6362

Jenny Lind (1820–87)

'Jenny Lind – the name carries music with it to English ears . . . For what is it which we have in our minds as we recall her name? It is, first, some tale of wonderful days when all London went mad over her singing. We have heard people tell, as their eyes kindle with the old passionate delight, how she came tripping over the stage in the Figlia, and how the liquid notes came rippling off her lips. We hear of the hours they waited in the historic crush at the Opera in the Haymarket . . .'
H.S. Holland and W.S. Rockstro in *Jenny Lind the Artist*, 1893

Steel engraving, Harry R. Beard Collection
L48

INDEX

Ellen Terry =

Larry Olivier

Edmund Kean

Peggy Ashcroft

Judi Dench

Sybil Thorndike

M. Forbes

Marie Lloyd

DAVID GARRICK.

Frederick Holl...